love All Faiths

Over One Thousand Three Hundred

 Questions and Answers on

Baha'i, Buddhism, Christianity,

Confucianism, Freemasonry, Hindus,

Islam, Jainism, Judaism, Mormons,

Paganism, Rastafarianism, Shinto,

Sikhism, Taoism, Zoroastrianism, God's

 Prophets BC

James Safo

James Safo's right as the researcher, author, designer of this publication to be identified and respected in accordance with the Copyright, Designs and Patent's Act 1988.

Disclaimer (Exclusive clause)

The author and all employees disclaim any incorrect interpretation wrong answers to questions or text, harm include emotional, psychological, and physical or any form of harm to the reader/listener or being given information by third parties.

Furthermore, this disclaimer protects all contributory people, directors, employees, 3 rd party, and author and will not be liable for any injury caused.

Who is   GOD
All religious faiths in the world worship
ONE GOD
Created heaven, all the planets
Universe) and everybody
And everything within.
GOD is
Alpha and Omega (beginning and
ending)
All knowing
All seeing
All hearing
The Great Architect of the universe
The Great Overseer of the universe
The Great Geometrician of the
universe
Almighty and Everlasting God
Sovereign God
Wisest Spirit, Invisible, Immortal.
God message through his
messengers is
          LOVE ALL FAITHS

Quick Search
Quick Search

Love All Faiths: Questions and Answers

Content of Individual Faiths

Name of faith	Approximate questions & answers	Chapter	Question pages	Answers pages
Baha'i	39	1	xxix–xxxi	1–7
Buddhism	103	2	xxxi–xl	8–58
Christianity	359	3	xl–lxviii	59–155
Confucianism	13	4	lxviii–lxix	156–159
Freemasonry	49	5	lxix–lxxiv	160–186
Hindus	156	6	lxxiv–lxxxiv	187–229
Islam	377	7	lxxxiv–cxv	230–350
Jainism	41	8	cxv–cxviii	351–358
Judaism	62	9	cxviii–cxxii	359–371
Paganism	38	10	cxxii–cxxiv	372–377
Shinto	21	11	cxxiv–cxxvi	378–381
Sikhism	66	12	cxxvi–cxxx	382–393
Taoism	20	13	cxxx–cxxxi	394–397
Zoroastrian	20	14	cxxxi–cxxxii	398–402

Preface

The aim of this book is to promote world peace through the understanding of other faiths. This, I hope, will help people to live together in harmony on earth before judgement day.

Faith/religion plays a major part in world peace. The reason being sometimes we tend to judge people superficially and might react unjustly.

We are afraid to ask questions in case the words and tone used offends people; we live in a world of uncertainty in most aspects of our behaviour in both verbal and non-verbal communication in how we pray and what we say in our prayers.

We claim to be monotheists (worship one God) but have different approaches.

Most of us draw conclusions and judge without understanding the ritual or motives of other faiths.

The tension between faiths could be reduced and make us approachable and sociable on earth.

If we are all believers who aim to go to Heaven, when the verdict of our behaviour, within God's Ten Commandments is delivered on the judgement day, we must start now to understand and live in peace on earth to prepare ourselves for the ultimate enlightenment.

God's Revenge

Believers are often disappointed to see their enemies or wicked people get away with their evil deeds. This has happened from time memorable and will never change.

God is very patient and will always welcome wicked people if they repent. Remember God loves everybody including lower animals and humans unconditionally. It is only in very exceptional circumstances that God will take revenge on wicked people.

The book of Psalm 91:8 says to righteous people, "You will see the reward of the wicked." The Oxford English Dictionary meaning of "reward" are all positive "something given in recognition of service, effort or achievement – honour, award."

For the believers who have gone through painful and suffering at the actions of wicked people, they find it difficult to comprehend and, in most cases, lose hope and faith. This is more so when believers during all their lives had been assured by the Holy books and faith leaders that God will take revenge on your enemies.

On the other hand, we need to pray for God's wisdom and knowledge.

How God takes revenge on enemies occurs in different forms, but it might not be what the individual wishes. The wicked could suffer emotionally. Outwardly they appear happy. My late mother told me, "You must not think that rich people or people you see walking on the street wearing expensive clothes or driving posh or sport cars are happy."

One assurance, as in Psalm 91, was that God grants protection from being killed or long-term injury, honours health and long life, which I can honestly support because I have had the experience during my journey.

On the question of reward and unconditional love, we know of murderers such as Moses who killed the Egyptians was the only person to see God's face (fire), the Ten Commandments from God was given to him for all mankind and he was also the one chosen to redeem the Israelites from the Egyptians. His only punishment was that he saw the promised land but never set foot upon it as he was buried outside the town Canaan.

Another example is Christian Apostle Saint Paul who killed thousands of Christians and was on his way to kill more when God made him blind; he recovered within 24 hours. His reward was that he became the most famous celebrity after Jesus. Paul was a typical example of how God protected him during his pain and suffering in prisons and house arrest just like me (James Safo).

In other cases, the wicked were swiftly punished. For example, Judas Iscariot committed suicide after he betrayed Jesus. Prophet Muhammad's neighbour who caused a lot of insult, harassment, poured rubbish into the prophet's property became ill and was helped by Prophet Muhammad. The three ruffians who killed Freemason founder, Master Mason were also killed. What about those wicked people not punished, for example the King's step daughter-in-law who caused the beheading of prophet John the Baptist?

Prophet Joseph's brothers who sold him to business men because of his interpretation of a dream which stated that the brother would one day bow to worship him. Or the woman who falsely accused Joseph of attempted rape, which then resulted in him having to serve a prison sentence for a long time.

God's revenge on groups of people have been through natural disasters. The Bible tells us that in Egypt when King Pharaoh persistently disobeyed God, he and the Egyptian people were punished. Because of the peoples' disobedience, God instructed Noah to build an Ark to save the righteous and God punished the sinners using flood water (it rained for forty days and nights taking the Ark to top of a mountain). There are many examples in the Holy books: Bible, the Quran, Bhagavat Gita, etc.

In modern times we have seen destruction by fire, water, air, earthquake or even human inventions turned against people.

I have experienced most of this, which my autobiography, poems and other books indicate my opinions on this subject. I, therefore, am not in a position to pass judgement on God's decision. I will only say: "Trust and have faith in God, be patient for his appointed time to answer one's supplication."

I sincerely hope this book will break the ice between various faiths to communicate without any apprehension of the outcome.

Acknowledgements

I had pondered on this topic for months with no answer to who inspired me to write about ten books plus my autobiography while in a constrained environment – prison. I had no hesitation to delete human beings from my list.

The real author of all my books is Almighty God/Allah/Parama Nandha through his messengers. I was not capable of neither writing books or achieving those high-power qualifications: Physically, 75% of my bones are in advanced arthritis, I have the worst cardiovascular disease, a large heart (hypertrophy), chronic depression and anxiety and, worst of all, three out of four of my brain lobes have been damaged since 1998.

Due to my miscarriage of justice, for eight years I have cried tears at least three times a day and every morning my pillows were wet from tears and my eyesight faded; as a result, I wear reading glasses and had to have eye drops for last three years in prison.

Yes, my hands wrote all the manuscripts books as per the knowledge that came to me; I read the appropriate chapters in the Holy books – Bible, Quran, Bhagavat Gita, and physiology books. Sometimes I woke up during the night and had to write new ideas down and then I expanded it later.

I regard myself as a slave of God or catalyst. Many people when they see the number of qualifications: degree and high-power Diplomas, plus the number of books and my battle in courts with top people who use their position of power and financial muscle they took from me, they say, "James, you are amazing." I prefer those people to say, "James, you have been blessed by Almighty God." My answer is unequivocal that it is clear evidence of God's powers. He can make the impossible possible." So please do not say good things about me. Please do me a favour: just PRAISE and thank God. I am happy that God has used me to demonstrate his endless power. Please refer to my autobiography for full details why the above statement. *"The Slave of God"*.

Human acknowledgement

My greatest thanks are to Mr Mirek Siba who was my business accountant for over 18 years and stood by me when I lost everything and became destitute. He has been a true friend and deserves to be my rock when everyone else left me.

The second human is Mrs Nicola Burrow who was chosen by Almighty God to be my PA (personal assistance/secretary), who typed most of the books. In about April 2017, two weeks after I had a vision which I interpreted to say my pain and suffering was nearly over, God led me to ask the prison librarian to get me a typist. Within three days, Nicola accepted the job. She typed about 14 of my books, including my autobiography and law book and most of my courts claims documents to the High Court. She put up with my depression, sometimes my confusing instructions or illegible handwriting. Any reasonable person would appreciate how difficult it is to be a PA for me in prison as I cannot be contacted by phone or Internet via email. She is very honest, reliable and excellent. She is three "P" (Patience, Persistence and Perseverance). Jesus said do not trust any human, but Nicola is an exception to such advice (what do you expect from God? Perfect time management). She deserves my highest human thanks – "Bravo".

Moral support

It is a shame that out of thousands of people, all over the world, who I have helped in different ways, none of them were available when I went to prison or must I repeat what my ex-wife said in her 2011 letter before she filed divorce papers, "You had been very good to so many people, but they are powerless to help you."

The exceptions are my brother, Sam Osei, who came from Ghana to visit me, my best friends, Bernadette Redmond (over 30 years friendship) and Valli Letchuman (over 20 years), Jane Nakuya, my sisters Larkarley, Larley and Mary, and two daughters, Kate and Kiahna. My four sons Emmanuel, Morgan, Edward and Elliot, were more affected by my miscarriage of justice but they came to visit and were at the end of the phone to give me a shoulder to cry on.

I would like to thank some of the prisoners at Parkhurst Prison in 2011/12, the faith leaders, prison officers, especially Ms Sims, Senior Prison Officer, My Freemason officers and the library at HMP Parkhurst (on the Isle of Wight 2011/2012) who all played major parts to start my research.

Research for the Book

During my research it was sad to hear that some people do not wish to read any other religious faith holy books, either by their own choice or maybe influenced by others who do not wish them to be confused.

It is also sad to learn that most Christians do not know the bible well and have different interpretations to Jesus Christ's parable teaching which is unfortunately because there are thousands of different denominations.

My original faith book covering most of major faiths consists of over two thousand pages. Due to the size, I created four main books namely: *Faith Unity* over 980 pages, *Love all Faith* over 450 pages of over 1,300 questions and Answers of all faith. I further crated *God Messengers before Christ* (400 pages). All these books have got various faiths valuable information which about 20% of believers who for some reason don't want to read about other faiths might reconsider to read these books.

I therefore decided to extract information from the huge book *Faith United* to produce four individual faith books, so the other 20% may read or listen to learn more about their own faith; namely *Allah Loves Islam, God Love Christianity, God Enlightened Buddhism* and *Parama Nandha Loves Hinduism.*

Furthermore, the world population consists of about 75% of believers in God who are Islam and Christians. My research revealed that these two faiths are descendants of one father (Abraham), whose wives Hagai (Islam; Prophet Muhammad), and Saira (Christianity; Jesus Christ) both have in their Holy Books: Bible and Quran the Ten Commandments and both believe the story of Prophet Moses. It is sad that both faiths appear to dislike each other without reading the other's doctrine.

To address this, I have written the book *Islam V. Christianity* over 450 pages quoting from both the Bible and the Quran to support my call for Unity among these two faith brothers. And to promote world peace on earth and to match to Heaven as brothers have accepted to live with their differences in peace. **I am preparing to**

offer my life as sacrifice for this mission which I sincerely believe that God wants the two faiths to live in harmony and to direct or publicly dissociate themselves from people who fail to abide by the Ten Commandments.

I do not know who I am, but I believe that considering I have suffered painful events for years equivalent to the pain that both Prophets "Job and Joseph" endured; being put in prison for miscarriage of justice for a long time, pain inflicted by the United Kingdom public servants, people in high positions, friends and in law family etc; I attempted suicide five times, suspect attempted to kill me in prison, physical and neurological and mental disabilities. Despite these God bestowed on me high power qualifications including honourable degrees, over ten diplomas and I wrote many books whilst in prison, experience, knowledge and wisdom. I invite my readers and listeners of audio to read my auto biography which is the biggest in my opinion in the world in this century.

My books encompassed all the revelations to Gods messengers/ prophets namely: the Bible the first five books; Moses was given the Ten Commandments, the old testaments, David received the revelation to write the book of Psalms, Jesus Christ came with the teaching from God as express in the old testament. Over five hundred years later humans continued to disobey God's commandment "Love" "forgive". God has given humans the last chance when He sent his last revelation "The Quran" through his last prophet Muhammad as a way of life for all humans in the whole world.

I would like to remind the whole world and nations that all God's revelations through his messengers including Moses, David, Jesus Christ, Prophet Muhammed, Lord Krishna, Guru Nanak, India messengers in Bhagavat Gita are there for the whole world to adhere to. The fact that God chose different people of origin do not matter. God created all of us with the same organs, red blood and we breathe the same air. The colour of the skin is only to differentiate which part of the world one comes from and in the eyes of God must not form barriers to love and live in harmony.

God loves and accepts the way that all faith worships and praises him, that is why He gave all humans free will. So please learn to live with your differences and leave judgement to God.

My books are just to remind you once again what God wants, which has not changed since Moses delivered the Ten Commandments to all nations. I sincerely hope all believers will pray for increase in faith, trust and belief in God. To love and forgive one another irrespective of one's faith. Lastly, to help unbelievers who wish to practice a faith to do so? Never attempt to persuade anyone to change his faith, as this will upset God.

Let us all work hard to bring world peace, do not be a hypocrite be genuine when doing God's mission.

About the Author

I was an abandoned child at the age of four for four years; I became a high-profile international entrepreneur based in England for over twenty-five years and owned ten different businesses at the same time, including international college etc., I was arguably one of the most successful black persons in Europe at the time, before my miscarriage of justice. After writing the books, three medical experts cast doubt on my conviction (miracle). My autobiography reveals my extraordinary journey as Slave of Allah. I am devoted to being a slave of God and to worship Him with any faith believer.

I am severely physically disabled with mental health and neurological problems. I was a Christian prior to my research to write this book, but I am now a believer in all faiths and attend worshipping places of different faiths.

I have a son, daughter-in-law and grand-daughter who practice Islam faith. I have friends from different faiths. For example, my best friends Valli Letchuman is Hindus and Bernadette Gibson is Christian.

I hope my readers and audio listeners will also read my other religious books, especially *Faith Unity, Love All Faiths* (which contains over one thousand three hundred questions and answers on about 12 religious' faiths). Considering my health problems, I consider this book to contain messages from God and this is not of my doing.

Since God created humans, he has sent messengers, including Moses with the Ten Commandments, David with the Psalms, Jesus teaching and the last messenger with the way of life, Muhammed with the Quran to deliver the way that humans were to follow, yet his commandments have been broken repeatedly.

I sincerely believe that what God wants is for all faiths to unit and live in harmony on earth as preparation for the judgement day. Hence my books are to help this wish of God. There is no doubt that all believers in God agree so let's work towards unconditional unity.

My Qualifications

I probably might be the oldest man to achieve Honourable open degree in law and account (financial and management) plus psychology and social science university level one; BA(Hons)open, Cert acct professional accountant, Diploma in business law and diploma in Safety management. All these qualifications were achieved within three years (2014—2017) at the age of 67. I was in a confined prison environment and had no access to the internet or other outside students. Nobody in the prison did these subjects at the time. I only had five telephone tutorials from the university tutor/professor for each model. I did 120 units instead of 60 units recommended per academic year, hence I completed these subjects in half the normal time. It would have taken at least seven years. Please see my other qualifications of which most were obtained when I was serving miscarriage of justice (three medical experts reports were not available at the trial and my first appeal supports my innocence).

I have physical, psychiatric and neurological disabilities but it was Almighty God's miracles not mine.

I am currently a student of LLM (Master of Laws), which I commenced in November 2018. The university is allowing me to undertake the course over two years, instead of the usual five years.

Love All Faiths: Questions and Answers

BA (Hons)open; Law & Accounts

Certificate in Education (teaching)

RMN (qualified mental nurse)

GN qualified general nurse)

Financial accountant

Management accountant

Book keeping (diploma)

Criminology (diploma)

Business law (level 4) level 5 is a

degree

(Consists of Employment

International law (level 4)

Public law consists of 1)

Constitutional law;

2) Judicial review and 3) European law

Criminal law

Tort law

Property law Torts/Damages, Agency,

Contract, European 1)

Equity and Trust law

Contract law

Immigration law adviser

Psychology

Social science

Safety Management (Diploma)

Script writing (TV, radio, stage and film)

Computer technician level 2 (all computers,

laptops, mobile phone Microsoft specialist one

printer, networking)

build and repair CISSCO cert.

Autobiography, biography and family history writing

Theology (Bible studies) diploma

Plumbing level 3

Business enterprise

Advance management

Advance food hygiene

Intermediate health and safety

Diploma in hypnotherapy

Counselling skill

Clait plus diploma level 1 and 2

New Clait diploma level 2

(computer)

ECDL level 2 (European licence)

NVQ trainer and assessor

External internal verifier

I was an international entrepreneur

for over 25 years

Currently a student of LLM (Master

of Laws),

started in November 2018

Below is the list of my books to be published soon if not yet published:

1. *"The One" Over 130 Poems* Copyright © 2018

2. *Faith United* Copyright © 2018

3. *Faith Unity* Copyright © 2018

4. *God Enlighten (Awaken) Buddhism* Copyright © 2018

5. *God Loves Christianity* Copyright © 2018

6. *God Messengers* Copyright © 2018

7. *In Search of Wisdom in Freemasonry* Copyright © 2018

8. *Islam v. Christianity* Copyright © 2018 P Copyright © 2018

9. *Love All Faiths: Over 1,300 Questions and Answers* Copyright © 2018

10. *Mood Disorder* Copyright © 2018

11. *Parama Nandha Loves Hinduism* Copyright © 2018

In process

12. *Autobiography* Copyright © 2018

13. *The Law (Over 1,500 Questions and Answers)*
    Copyright © 2018

14. *Sweat and sour woman*   Copyright © 2018

15. *Business Law* Copyright © 2018

16. *No Money to Establish Business* Copyright © 2018

17. *Management Account*   Copyright © 2018

18. *Financial Account*   Copyright © 2018

19. *Blacks Great* Copyright © 2018

20. *Miscarriage of Justice*   Copyright © 2018

21. *Biggest Drug Trafficking in the UK (includes chapters of drugs mis-use, alcoholics, addiction and counselling)*

22. *"The Maze of British Justice System" – Miscarriage of Justice*

Contents

xxxvi

xl

Christian Science Church

Quakers

Baptist Church

I

Love All Faiths: Questions and Answers

c

Forgiveness

Angels

Inheritance in The Quran

Jesus and Ibrahim

cxxix

Chapter 1

Baha'i

1. **Q: How do Baha'i's regard God?**

    A: They believe that God revealed himself as humans in different countries.

2. **Q: Who was the messenger that God revealed himself to?**

    A: Baha'u'llah was the messenger. He taught both spiritually and socially.

3. **Q: What is Baha'i philosophy?**

    A: That there is only one God, one religion and one family, the unity of all faiths.

4. **Q: How many prayers a day is compulsory?**

    A: There are three. A short prayer between 12 midday to 6p.m., then a medium prayer between 6p.m. to 9p.m and a longer prayer once in 24 hours.

5. **Q: What is the posture that individuals should adopt?**

A: Stand facing the shrine of Baha'u'llah and recite in silence and they must recite "Allah-u-Abha" which means God is most glorious – 95 times within 24 hours.

6.   **Q: Are there any restrictions on diet?**

A: No alcohol, some are vegetarians but no restrictions in diet, dress or headwear.

7.   **Q: How many months are there to a Baha year?**

A: It has 19 months at 19 days each and no allocated day of worship, although some communities meet the first day of their month.

8.   **Q: Do they fast?**

A: Yes. From 2nd to 20th March (sunrise to sunset).

9.   **Q: Do Baha'i's have Holy days?**

A: Yes, from 26th February to 1^{st}March and these Holy days are called Ayyam-i-Hà.

10.   **Q: Who founded Baha'i and when?**

A: Syyid 'Ali-Muhammad nicknamed "Bab" means the Gate in 1844.

11.   **Q: What was his philosophy?**

2

A: He had a vision of the God's messenger coming to judge all humans.

12. **Q: What happened to him?**

A: He was persecuted, tortured and was killed.

13. **Q: Who was Mirza Hussayn-Ali?**

A: He was the follower of Bab who was put in prison "Black Pit" dungeon for at least four months, he was tortured in the worst prison in Tehran, Iran where he had a vision.

14. **Q: What was the vision?**

A: In 1863 he said that he had a revelation that he was the prophet foretold by Bab when he had been exiled to Baghdad.

15. **Q: What name did Mirza adopt?**

A: Baha'u'llah meaning Glory of God.

16. **Q: Because of announcing his vision what happened next?**

A: In 1868 he was exiled to Adrianople, then wrote letters to world leaders to solve their differences and used their position of power for world peace.

17. **Q: What was his faith?**

A: He revealed this in a Holy book called Kitab-I-Aqdas meaning *The Most Holy Book*.

18. **Q: What is the main faith or doctrine?**

A: It was unity and avoid discrimination, prejudice, persecution or conflict; know and worship God. There is no priesthood or worship.

19. **Q: When and how do they meet?**

A: They meet once every 19 days for feast and worship (this includes prayers) and socialising.

20. **Q: How can one recognise their house of worship?**

A: It has nine sides and a central dome, to mean unity for humanity.

21. **Q: What do you see inside?**

A: Symbols of most of the world's faiths.

22. **Q: What do they do when they meet every 19 days?**

A: They have a discussion of community concerns, including housing benefits, education.

23. **Q: Where is the largest group?**

A: In India.

24. **Q: Where did the Baha'i originate?**

4

A: In Iran.

25. **Q: What are the two traditions and their meaning?**

   A: Bab means the gate and Baha'u'llah, which means the glory of God.

26. **Q: Who founded the Baha'i?**

   A: The founder was Mirza Husayn-Ali (1817–92).

27. **Q: Who was he, another Muhammad?**

   A: He was a rich man who refused a political cabinet position. He used his money to help the poor and followed Bab. He was imprisoned where he had followers, after claiming in 1852 that he had a vision as Messenger of God. Then he was released and in 1863 the Baha'i was born.

28. **Q: Why do you like Baha'i?**

   A: I do respect all monotheism faiths and any philosophies who practice forgiveness, believe, trust and love as per the Ten Commandments.

29. **Q: Come on, James. Tell us why.**

   A: I have told you. Go away, Satan.

30. **Q: OK. What do they believe?**

A: Unity of all mankind. That the earth is but one country, and mankind its citizens.

31. **Q: Any other beliefs?**

A: They believe that the major religion credited to some individuals were teachers sent by God.

32. **Q: Name some of these?**

A: Abraham, Buddha, Gobind Singh, Krishna, Jesus Christ, Moses, Muhammad, Zoroaster, etc.

33. **Q: What were Baha'i laws?**

A: They are: "This is in line with God's Ten Commandments." They believe in equality, avoid prejudice, discrimination, eliminate poverty, and encourage other rich people to help the poor.

34. **Q: Anything else?**

A: I know what your (Satan) evil mind is looking for.

35. **Q: Please tell me.**

A: I cannot tell you all, it may take years to do so, but one main theme is members are to search for the truth.

36. **Q: Yes, I have got you. The founder appears to compare himself to Buddha – wandering about searching for the truth.**

A: A… (Satan started again) no comment.

37. **Q: You said earlier that the founder declared himself as the long-awaited messenger of God, like Prophet Muhammad.**

A: You are entitled to your opinion but all of them (faith) support tolerance of different views, world unity and justice and spiritual essence, the same.

38. **Q: Who succeeded him?**

A: His eldest son, Abbas Effendi (Abdu'l-Baha). Unbeliever: O yes – keep it in the family like the British monarch.

39. **Q: How many followers?**

A: At least seven million – Canada, USA, Mexico, South America, Africa, Europe, Asia, Australia.

Chapter 2

Buddhism

40.   **Q: What is the Buddhism view about doubt?**

A: Doubt is a hindrance. It could lead to understanding of truth and spiritual progress.

Doubt is not a "sin" because there is no article of Faith in Buddhism.

Buddhists believe the root of all evil is ignorance and false views.

To progress in life Buddhists must not have any doubt, perplexity or wavering (this is supported by Jesus, Muhammed and Krishna – for spiritual growth).

It is however, accepted as a Buddhist to have doubt if one doesn't understand or see clearly to force oneself to believe and to accept a thing without understanding is political and not spiritual or intellectual.

Buddhists must always dispel doubt.

41. **Q: What are Buddhists views of other religion?**

A: Buddhists must have freedom of thought and tolerance and understanding. This can be supported when Emperor Asoka of India in the third century BC honoured and supported all other religions in his vast empire.

Failure for Buddhists to accept all religion will result in digging your own grave and causing injuries to yourself.

42. **Q: What is Buddhism view on violence?**

A: Buddhism is absolutely against violence in any form, under any pretext whatsoever.

43. **Q: Is Buddhism a religion or a way of life/philosophy?**

A: The answers were conflicting. Most Buddhists said a label is immaterial and that labels are a hindrance to understanding of the truth and can produce prejudice in the mind.

44. **Q: What is truth?**

A: Buddhists view that, it does not matter the source and development of truth or idea. They claim it is the matter of academicia. You do not need to know where the teaching comes from.

45. **Q: How does one prepared to become Buddhist?**

A: To be ordained as Buddhist you must have alms, bowl and robes. You will also need to have a guru to teach you the laws and way of Buddhist.

46. **Q: How does a Buddhist regard the word faith?**

A: Buddhism emphasise on SEEING, knowing and understanding and NOT FAITH or BELIEF.

Buddhists prefer to use CONFIDENCE or DEVOTION instead of FAITH.

In the fourth century, Asanga – the great Buddhist philosopher classified Faith (SNADDHA) into three aspects: (1) Full and firm conviction that a thing is; (2) Serene joy at good qualities; and (3) Aspirations or wishes to achieve an object.

47. **Q: How do Buddhist explain belief?**

A: Buddhists do not like to use the word BELIEF because belief is something one has not seen and that will cause doubt. They refer to Jesus's disciple Thomas who refused to accept the resurrection until he saw the wound in Jesus's hand.

Buddhists prefer to use the phrase "Realised Truth" i.e. the eye has confirmed the truth. Buddha said, "It is always seeing through knowledge or wisdom and not believing through Faith."

Orthodoxy believe without seeing because they have heard from historians of people who have witnessed or seen the miracles of God, Jesus, Krishna, Vishnu, Prophets and Muhammad.

48. **Q: What is the aim of Buddhist doctrine?**

A: The whole Buddhist doctrine is meant to lead a man to safety, peace, happiness, tranquillity and to attain maturity as Buddhist.

49. **Q: How do Buddhists achieve their aim?**

A: Having spoken to a few Buddhists, it was reported that Buddha's answer to metaphysical questions (such as is the universe finite or infinite? Is the earth round?) was, "Do not worry about what you have not seen." He continued, "Many millions are wasting their valuable time on such metaphysical questions and unnecessarily disturbing their peace of mind."

50. **Q: What was Buddha's view on science?**

A: It was clear that when Buddhists don't know an answer to a question because they have not seen as they term "REALISATION OF TRUTH" the Buddha commented, "I have not explained because it is not useful, is not fundamentally connected to aversion, detachment, cessation, tranquillity, deep penetration full realisation." (The Buddha was reported to have said this to a young man called Malunkya-Putta).

51. **Q: Why Buddhism dislike using the words *FAITH, SIN, TRUST, WORSHIP*. What is faith in Buddhism?**

A: There are conflicting answers.

Some Buddhists have faith but in truth or faith in the four Noble Truths.

Others think Faith is blind, that belief needs the existence of evidential matter, no matter how small or remote. Belief because you have reason to think or know it is true. Faith is where you take it as the truth based on no evidence or because of previous evidence not related to the matter in point now, i.e. taking someone's word for something is Faith based upon your BELIEF in the person. (How would you know if they lie?)

52. **Q: What is SIN in Buddhism?**

A: Some Buddhists think "sin" is a religious concept. Others think sin is just another word for moral law.

In Buddhism, there is a moral code, the natural language of the cosmos. A person cannot escape their karma: they can realise the truth of their own actions and train to remove wrong action. Even though they must still accept their karma, which may bring them even more suffering and an almost insurmountable challenge (e.g. Angulimala).

53. **Q: What is trust in Buddhism?**

A: Some use the word trust to mean confidence in the truth or reliability of something or someone.

Others believe that you should question everything to find your own path or answer, hence you do not trust anyone.

54. **Q: What is worship in Buddhism?**

A: Some Buddhism's do not use the word worship because is a religious concept. They believe in following, copying and giving are to them synonyms of worship.

Some Buddhism seek truth and balance. They respect and honour the Buddha and the teachings they discover.

They regard all things as either equal or equally important or of equal insignificance. Worship is regarded as devotion to something outside of us. Buddha's nature is discovered within. That which is around Buddhists are within them. To worship Buddha would be to worship individual concerns – which is an act of pride the force, they humbly respect and honour.

14

55. **Q: What do we mean by spiritual progress since Buddhism do not believe in spirit?**

A: Spiritual progress is used to describe the essence of things, that which is …. and unsullied. By the crossing of physical attachment.

Other interpretations: any reference to a spirit or spirituality is used in some books because there is no direct and exact way to express the "Pali" (language) terms in English to a world that only understands religious concepts.

56. **Q: Since Buddhism believe in reincarnation of an individual force, has the founder Buddha re-existed?**

A: The essence or energy or life that one can be reincarnated in another (body) vehicle has seven chances to reach the final stage of human journey, i.e. Fourth Noble Truth "The Enlightenment", the individual (body) is NOT reincarnated.

Buddha reached the Enlightenment at the age of 35 and taught for 45 years until he died at 80.

Another answer I got was: Buddha is reported to have said that he had lived before and that when he was born to the kingdom this was his Final reincarnation and that he would not be reborn again.

*Reincarnation-Transmission of life – essence with Kama to new VEHICLE.

57. **Q: Buddhism talk about evil. Do you believe in Satan?**

A: "Evil" in Buddhist practice is morally wrong. They feel that evil is a word that represents the opposite to good. Evil is not religious. SATAN is regarded as RELIGIOUS as the mythical representation of a person in opposition to mythical God.

Buddhists believe there are good and bad people. Some are bad enough to use the technical term evil but that does not make them Satan. These people have strayed very far from the middle path and are lost and in great need of someone to bring them back.

Buddhism do not believe in the existence of Satan, angel, saint, prophets or god.

58. **Q: If Buddhism's don't like to use the word worship, why do they have status in books and premises?**

A: Difference of opinion or interpretation. A statue of Buddha represents his presence in the world centuries ago and serves Buddhists and as a symbol of the fact that ordinary man, through searching TRUTH in meditation, can attain ENLIGHTENMENT. Other status's or items represent various aspects of wisdom and natural law.

Another answer was status and Slupa's mark places where the earth's energy "chi" is at its most easily available or strongest. These are sign posts of where Buddhists can upload or download "kama" self-most readily. These statues are not meant to be worshipped, just gathered around. Those less capable of generating their own energy need a place for help.

59. **Q: How accurate is the written text of Buddha teaching?**

A: We are told that Buddha was born (sixth century) 563BC and died eighty years later. The records revealed that there was no written record of his teaching recorded until three months after his death when a council of his disciples met to draft his teaching in "Pali" language. Nothing was done until the first century BC (found 450 years later) before a group of scholars met to write the doctrine.

My research revealed that not all the teaching of Buddha has been discovered up to now.

One Buddhist, Wayne Eaton, said, "The first written words were found by non-Buddhist in First century bc. They were written and put away in many hiding places after being created. As with anything these are the views of others and should not be taken as FAITH." He continued, "Live by the words, by doing then you can judge how accurate the old words are."

60.   **Q: The fourth noble truth of Buddhism stated that total enlightenment means the person has achieved cessation. Why do some books claim that Buddha reincarnated?**

A: One experienced Buddhist agreed that after reaching the cessation (Enlightenment) there will be no reincarnated again.

Another experienced Buddhist Mark Sulton stated, "Buddha reached perfection in his final incarnation. It is important that it is understood that this was Siddhartma Gautama Buddha 'Buddha' means fully Enlightenment one." He went on, "Anyone can become Buddha. Some Buddhists are given a choice upon becoming Enlightenment (cessation) to NIRVANA or Bonhisattva – remaining within the world to teach (MAHAYANAN BUDDHISM) – THERAVADAN or slick to cessation concept.

61.   **Q: Buddhism claim that when someone dies, the energy or force within that person is transferred to the next generation. Transfer to what vehicle?**

A: "Reincarnation will continue whether it be into a human body, animal, insect, fish, tree, grass (different schools of Buddhism have different ideas on this. Some say humans cannot reincarnate as anything but humans).

If you reach the end of your seventh life and have still not achieved Enlightenment the energy will then pass to a new vehicle (living thing) but as a newly erased, cleansed, energy force that has no connection with the energy that used to be you. You will no longer exist in any form and what was your energy may now be another vehicle (tree, bird, insect or ant). that is something that can never ever be enlightened.

62.   **Q: The body dies and decays. There is no soul but the force within the body reincarnates into another form. This continues until the force is cut off through wisdom which sees reality, truth – how?**

A: The force is an energy and energy never ceases. It only changes. The name given to this energy is consciousness.

20

Upon enlightenment [(the end) (the cut off)] this energy becomes another form of energy. Before enlightenment, the energy enters another consciousness. This is commonly called reincarnation by the Western World.

63.   **Q: Am I right to say only Buddhists who reach Enlightenment life ends when he dies? If so why do people say Buddha reincarnated?**

A: When Buddha reached the Enlightenment, he had the choice for rebirth. It is possible because he was the one who the people believed and followed, that he chose to rebirth to continue his teaching.

64.   **Q: When is a Buddhism path reached?**

A: The path is reached by ceasing evil, cultivating good, cleansing your mind by living in virtue. This allows a clear mind that can meditate and so find wisdom. Cleanse your mind by ceasing greed, hatred and ignorance.

65.   **Q: What is satisfactoriness?**

A: Satisfactoriness is made up of five aggregates which is matter, feeling, perception, mental and consciousness.

66. **Q: How do these aggregates work?**

A: The first four are human senses (sight, smell, sound, taste, touch) plus information from the mind.

67. **Q: Explain consciousness?**

A: Consciousness is only ever in the mind and has no connection with the outside influence? It lives from now onward. So you can still remember what the senses (pain) have picked up.

68. **Q: How does meditation work?**

A: Meditation shuts out the senses that process outside influences and allows for total concentration of the consciousness.

69. **Q: What is mind change?**

A: Change comes about by becoming aware of the need to change, accept what is not right and needs changing, and find the desire to make it happen and act. This requires both effort

22

and path (direction). No matter how much effort you put in it is not useless, if it is in the right direction.

70.   **Q: What is life and death?**

A: Life is just a transfer of energy and energy can only change, not cease to exist, so death is a transfer to another existence, not a cessation.

71.   **Q: How does this reincarnation stop?**

A: According to Buddhism, the only way to achieve cessation is by gaining total enlightenment, then reaching Nirvana. Nirvana is total and complete perfection or bliss and can therefore never be explained to anyone that has yet to feel it as no words can convey pure satisfaction.

72.   **Q: What follows happiness?**

A: From happiness comes unhappiness but knowing it will come minimises its effect. Do not be pessimistic or optimistic, be realistic.

73.   **Q: What does forgiveness mean to Buddhism?**

A: Forgiveness, whether it is of self or of another, releases both from being held in the past and so fighting against change. The future is made in the present not in the past. By hanging on to items or events from the past you are binding yourself to the past and so not allowing yourself to live in the present and create the future.

74. **Q: How does one deal with fear (Buddhism way)?**

A: Fear must make you stronger to overcome fear. If you are weak and shy away from the fear, you will need to face it again some time. According to Buddha teaching, the best way to deal with fear is to be strong by following the eightfold path of: right understanding, thought, speech, action, livelihood, effort, mindfulness and concentration.

1. Understanding + Thought (attitude) brings WIDSOM.

2. Speech, Action + Livelihood brings MORAL CORRECTNESS.

3. Effort, Mindfulness + Concentration enable MEDITATION.

75. **Q: Why would Buddhism not use belief?**

A: Buddhism prefer to use the word realisation not belief. If you need belief, then you have not seen and do not "know" which leaves room for doubt.

76. **Q: Formula**

A:

1. Right Understanding + Right Attitude = WISDOM.

2. Right Speech + Right Mindfulness + Right Livelihood = MORALS.

3. Right Effort + Right Mindfulness + Right Concentration = CONCENTRATION.

4. Wisdom + Morals + Concentration will get rid of greed, anger and ignorance = GOOD PERSON.

77. **Q: As Buddha was a prince, was it possible that he might have felt proud to admit his wisdom came from a supernatural being?**

A: Buddha renounced all claims to the throne, all possessions and all ties to his family when he left his father's palace at the age of 29. He had come to realise that wealth, luxury, title and worldly power would not bring peace to a person's heart. More significantly, that those things would not bring an end to the suffering of the human condition. Before leaving the palace in this way, he had already journeyed beyond the walls of the Palace grounds, without his father's knowledge or permission, and witnessed disease, old age, dreams and acetic monkhood. These observations strengthened his resolve to find a way to end human suffering, hence his renunciation of possessions, title, wealth and luxury.

Buddha believed one of the causes of human suffering was the ego which gives rise to selfishness, greed, pride, fear, to name but a few. These emotions, in consultation with a strong ego, leads to great suffering, not only for the individual experiencing them, but also to those

26

around them. Buddha realised this, and it is expressed in the first noble truth (Buddha's teaching). There is suffering, note the non-personal aspect of this statement. It is not "I am suffering" or "you are suffering". It is detached from individuals without the ego, without possession of the suffering. It is something we all experience, just as we all seek to be happy. Therefore, to realise the way to end the suffering of the ego must be let go of. Hence greed, selfishness, pride and fear are also let go of. Buddha did not deny the existence of supernatural powers, he merely stated that it was only through personal effort that one can come to realise the truth. One does not work for oneself, he said that Buddha's natural picture was of unintentional existence in all things throughout the universe and it was up to individuals to work to discover this within oneself.

Hence if Buddha still had pride, he could not have had the ability to put forth his teaching the way he did.

Buddha nature – the word Buddha means "The Enlightenment" which pervades throughout everything.

78. **Q: What were the religions in his kingdom at that time?**

A: His father was the ruler of the Shakya Clan, who lived along the Rohini river among the southern foothills of the Himalayas, part of the region now known as India. At that time, various schools or Vedic philosophy/theology were the prominent religions of the Aru, the philosophy's/theologies that are the root of Hinduism, among other religions, to emerge from those schools of thought.

79. **Q: Did Buddha become the king when his father died?**

A: No, he renounced his title of prince and the line of succession passed to another member of the family.

80. **Q: At that time how did they calculate the age?**

A: He was 29-years-old when he left the palace, 35-years-old when he became enlightened and 80 when he died.

During his 45 years of teaching, Buddha taught many disciples, many of whom attained a high level of Enlightenment, and who spent a lot of time with him, so they knew him well. Shortly after Buddha's death, it was decided amongst his disciples that it was possible that errors may come into the transmission of the Buddha teaching if they just continued as individuals passing on what they each understood of his teachings. So many senior Monks, who had all known Buddha personally, including Ananda, the Buddha's closest disciple, discussed Buddha's teaching and his life, over several months. This was to ensure that they were correct in their transmission of his life and teachings, and those were written down at that time, forming the original written *Dharma*, the body of teaching and the life of the Buddha. Therefore, Buddhism knew his age at various stages of his life so accurately, they were recorded by a group of people who had known him personally and a long time, shortly after his death.

81. **Q: It can be argued that his life was never in danger because he was within his father's kingdom compared to Jesus, Muhammad, Moses, David and other prophets.**

A: This may be true, but the question is who of us is not in danger? We are all subject to suffering, we are all vulnerable to disgrace, pain, injury, both mentally and physically. We are all going to die. Most of us at some time in our lives will experience death of someone we love. Just being alive is a dangerous condition. This was no different for the Buddha. His mother died after he was born and his aunt Mahaprajapti became his foster mother. He perceived the vulnerability of the human condition, and rather than choosing to hide against the trappings of the life of a prince: being wealthy, well-fed and being well-entertained with distractions from worldly worries, he chose the life of a beggar and monk, possessing only a robe, a begging bowl, and followed the life of and teaching prominent ascetic monks, who practised a life of extremes. There was very little food, no entertainment, prolonged and often painful periods of meditation and denial of life's so-called pleasures. Buddha did this by choice; it was not forced upon him. He did become very weak and close to death through these practises occasionally.

After his Enlightenment, some religious people did feel threatened by the strength of his following and in most parts upon meeting him, found they could not fault his reasoning, and became his disciples. There were understandably times when his life was threatened. One such occasion was his meeting with Angulimala. Buddha sensed he was needed in a nearby forest which was the hunting ground of a much-feared bandit, Angulimala, who was famous for wearing a necklace of fingers from the many people he had murdered. He attacked and killed anyone he came across in the forest he lived in, taking a finger and their possessions. Buddha sensed that Angulimala's mother was travelling in the forest and knew that Angulimala would kill him without recognising her as his mother. So, Buddha went to the forest to confront Angulimala before he came across his mother. Angulimala saw Buddha and tried to attack him but Buddha was never where Angulimala attacked. He tried again and again, every time Buddha evaded the attack effortlessly until Angulimala tired and exacerbated, exclaimed to Buddha, "How do you move so fast?" Buddha replied, "I am standing still, it is you who cannot stop running." On hearing these words Angulimala saw wisdom in Buddha, and begged to become his disciple, which meant him renouncing his former life of crime. So, in many ways Buddha did experience danger and opposition. It is worth noting that Angulimala's life was not easy as a disciple, as he travelled, he was recognised many times. He never retaliated, he was prepared to accept his Kama (self), the result of his deeds before becoming a monk.

82. **Q: Is it possible that politics might have played part of his popularity as his father's kingdom is where he was operating?**

A: By all accounts, it was the wisdom of his teaching that gave him the followers. It is also true to say that there was no animosity between him and his father, he visited his father after the Enlightenment and his father respected his son's path, but Buddha had no say in the governing of the region and had no power in that way. His father had not wished for his son to become a monk, he wanted him to rule after him and did not fully understand Buddha's way of life. Buddha's father, Shuddmodana Gautama, was by all accounts a benevolent ruler. His people did not suffer under his rule, neither did they lack the necessities of life. So, there were no political gains for someone in becoming a disciple of Buddha. Perhaps some did initially follow him because of his heritage but this would have been apparent in their demeanour, and Buddha and/or his higher-ranking disciples would have spotted this farce commitment and would have endeavoured to teach them the falsehood of seeking worldly gain or power.

83.   **Q: What was the religious faith in the palace before Buddha left the palace?**

A: There were many Vedic schools in the Arga, mostly led by monks, commonly known as Yogis, and it is almost certain their beliefs were that of one of those Vedic schools of thought. Within six years of leaving the palace and attaining the enlightenment, Buddha sought knowledge from the most highly regarded ascetic monks of the region and became a disciple of two of them for several years. Buddha said that although he understood these teachings he did not feel that they gave the complete answer which was when he left all the teachers and sought the ultimate knowledge by himself.

84.   **Q: Buddhism's do not accept the Holy Spirit or any other spirit within them. Instead they**

use the word *energy* or *power* within the body. Why?

A: Some Buddhists feel that *force* is not the word used to express the aspect of the human condition. They think that it may have been over simplified in translation. Some have heard *power* being used but they think the connotations of the word in English are misleading. Others say *energy* may be a better word or the Chinese word *Chi*, expressing the life force that animated living things that are present, in Buddhist thinking, throughout all things. It is also called Buddha-nature.

In an individual, the thoughts and actions of that individual effect the nature of the *Chi* within them. It can become clouded and weakened by incorrect attitudes and actions, that is against the natural low of the universe. This accumulation is known as Kama. A person with Kama needs to clean themselves out, work out their Kama, purify and hence strengthen their internal energy, and hence arrive at their true, clear, essential nature, regarded as Enlightenment. In Buddhism, this energy is what is transferred in reincarnation. Whatever the state of that energy at the time of death, it is transferred on to another vehicle as it is containing the pure essence of life (Buddha-natures) and may accumulate Kama. Hence it is always possible for an individual to rediscover their Buddha-nature, but they must work out their Kama before they can see clearly. Once the life force is clear, pure, it can either re-join with the cosmic consciousness or choose to be reborn in a physical vehicle as a teacher.

Since Buddhism, especially Tibetan Buddhism, believe theirs is a third place, the spirit world where energy exists independent of a physical vehicle, and that these energies can be in many states: pure Buddha-nature and mixed Buddha-nature with Kama. These are something regarded as "Gods" but are not regarded as God in the Christian sense imbued with ruler-ship of the universe and control of a person's soul, rather as just another state of existence.

85. **Q: Why do Buddhists not like to use faith, sin, trust worship?**

A: Faith – Buddhists have faith – faith in the truth.

Sin is just another word for the breaking of moral law. In Buddhism, there is a moral code. The natural laws of the cosmos, breaking them giving a person Kama – a person cannot escape their Kama: they can realise the truth of their own actions and train to remove wrong actions, but even then, they must still accept their Kama, which may bring them great suffering and/or almost insurmountable challenges (e.g. Angulimala).

Trust – Buddhists use the word trust – trust is confidence in the truth or reliability of something or someone.

Worship – we seek truth and balance, we respect and honour the universe, us, Buddha and the teachings he discovered. All things are equal – of equal importance and of equal insignificance. Worship is devotion to something outside us. Buddha-nature is discovered within. That which is around us is within us – to worship Buddha would be to worship ourselves – an act of pride, therefore, we humbly respect and honour instead.

Faith is blind. Belief needs the existence of evidential matter, no matter how small or remote. Belief is because you have reason to think/know it is true. Faith is where you take it as true based on no evidence or because of previous evidence not related to the matter in point now, i.e. taking someone's word for something is *faith* based upon your *belief* in that person. If they lie you would not know.

Sin is a religious concept.

Buddha believed that you should question everything to find your own path or answer and therefore you do not need to *trust*.

Worship is a religious concept. Believe in/following/copying/giving; these would replace worship.

86. **Q: Buddhists don't like the word worship. Why do you have so many statues in books? and premises?**

A: Statues of Buddha represents his presence in the world centuries ago and serves as a symbol of the fact that ordinary man through *seeking* truth in meditation can attain enlightenment. Other items represent various aspects of wisdom and natural law.

Statues and Stupa's mark places where the earth's energy, *Chi*, is at its most easily available or strongest. These are signposts of where you can upload or download Kama most readily. They are not there to be worshipped, just gathered around for those less capable of generating their own energy need a place for help.

87. **Q: Buddha lived in the sixth century. According to Buddhism, the council of his disciples met three months after his death to draft some of the teachings. It was not until the first century BC before the first written**

**copy was made (450 years after his death).
How accurate is it of what we read now?**

A: It was written by the council and later rediscovered.

The first written words were found by a non-Buddhist in the first century BC. They were written and put away in many hiding places after being created. As with anything else these are the views of others and should not be taken on *faith*. Live by the words, try out the teachings, find your own *belief* by doing so, then you can judge how accurate the old words are.

88. **Q: When one achieves total enlightenment, this means He has achieved cessation. Why did some Buddhist books claim that Buddha? had reincarnated?**

A: Buddha reached perfection in his final incarnation. It is important that it is understood that this was Siddhartha Gautama Buddha. "Buddha" means fully enlightened one. Anyone can become a Buddha.

Some Buddhists believe choice upon enlightenment – cessation (Nirvana) or Bodhisattva – remaining within the world to teach (Mahayana Buddhism – Theravada – stick to cessation concept).

Enlightenment means the cessation of the cycle. You will not be reincarnated again after you have reached enlightenment. I assume the book you mention means *before* his enlightenment.

89. **Q: The Buddhism teaching said, "Death is a transfer of energy to another existence *unless* the person had reached total enlightenment. Therefore a perfect person like Buddha and possible. Blessing one other will lose their energy when they die. Please explain?**

A: See answer to 7.

Reincarnation is continuous until enlightenment, whether it be into a human, animal, insect, fish, tree or grass (different schools of Buddhism have different ideas on this

41

– some say humans cannot reincarnate as anything but humans).

Yes, death is an energy transferred into another vehicle unless you reached enlightenment during this life 1–6. At this "death" you will, or your energy will move to Nirvana but will still exist just in a different form that none of us can understand or imagine.

If you reach the end of your seventh life and have still not achieved enlightenment the energy will then pass to a new vehicle but as a new, erased, cleansed, energy force that has no connection with the energy that used to be you. You will no longer exist in any form and what was your energy may now be a tree, a flower, a bird, an ant, something that cannot ever be enlightened. This is how I understand it. thankfully, as a tree, flower, bird etc. others who are still trying to become enlightened can still use the new you to learn from so nothing is wasted.

90. **Q: A book of Buddhism stated: Teachers of Buddhism were "God" or Buddha**

42

reincarnated in a different form or inspired by God. Please explain?

A: See answer to 7.

Footnote – Buddha stressed in his teachings that most important to a person is their own actions and path – if one perfect living in this world then all else follows. He felt that preoccupation with meta-physical concepts were mostly irrelevant to one's progress and a distraction. Understanding of the meta-physical is a natural by-product of enlightenment, but is? not necessary to achieve enlightenment. Therefore, other worlds, other realms of existence, what happens after we die, the existence or non-existence of God are all irrelevant to us and a distraction from living in the present moment with true clarity.

Buddha rarely *spoke* of his thoughts on the existence of a Creator – God. He did once say that if such a being existed, why would he create suffering, but he never definitively denied or confirmed the existence of a Creator – God, but most scholars (Buddhists and otherwise) agreed that his teachings implied that he didn't believe in a Creator – God.

If someone performs a good action to get benefits for themselves – if they are thinking, "If I do this I will have more chance of becoming enlightened" or "If I do this I will have a greater chance to enter Heaven," the action is not a pure good action, it is self-serving. A good action should be done purely because it is good, with no thought of God or a reward.

There is a story of one day in Buddha's life a man who had spent his whole life believing in a Creator – God symbolised by the sun, was approaching death and began to doubt if God existed. He had heard of Buddha and decided to ask him. He saw him early in the morning and asked if God existed. Buddha said, "No." Buddha's disciples who overheard were overjoyed that Buddha had finally given a definitive statement about the existence of God and ran around telling the other disciples. Later the same day, another man who had spent his whole life believing there was no Creator – God, and who was also approaching death began to wonder if he was wrong and had heard of Buddha and decided to ask him. In the evening, he found Buddha and asked. Buddha said, "Yes." The disciples were confused, why had Buddha given a different answer to each man? The answer was that he was challenging each man to look at themselves and question the nature of their own beliefs.

Again, I do not know why certain things are written in certain ways in certain books. I would expect it is due to errors in translation and the writer trying to find a representation that the Western world could understand easily. In the West, we can visualise what is meant by God but the idea of a superior being is seen in a negative way. In the East, it is readily accepted that many people are greater than normal or average and these people are good and beneficial.

91.   **Q: What is the meaning of Buddha?**

A: A Buddha who has reached expectation is called "One who knows" or "The Enlightened One".

92. **Q: What is the main doctrine of Buddhism?**

A: To know the problem of suffering and to end it.

93. **Q: How do they gain perfection?**

A: Buddhists go through gradual training of perfection of virtue, meditation and that leads eventually to wisdom "Enlightenment".

94. **Q: What underpins Buddhist's principles?**

A: There are five: that a person must not kill, steal, sexual misconduct, unfaithfulness, avoid alcohol and illegal drugs.

95. **Q: Do Buddhists believe in God?**

A: No, they are non-theistic – they do not believe in a creator or Messiah or God.

96. **Q: What do Buddhists believe in?**

A: They do not use the word *believe* or *faith*. They believe that no soul, no self is binding.

97. **Q: If Buddhists do not use belief or faith, what is their phenomenon?**

A: That all humans arise depending on causes and conditions without substance, one's intentions, actions and rebirth when one dies.

98. **Q: What qualities do we expect from a Buddhist?**

A: Faithfulness, patience, generosity, loving-kindness, compassion, non-attachment.

99. **Q: What do they aim at?**

A: They aim to purify the mind and suffering, and eventually Nirvana (stop rebirth).

100. **Q: What are their Holy days?**

A: There are six main Holy days:

1. Theravada – New or full moon
2. Magha Puja or Sangha day
3. Visakha Puja or Wesak or Buddha Day, which is Buddha's birthday
4. Pavarana Day (Sangha Day)
5. Asalha Puja (Dhamma Day)
6. Mahayana.

101. **Q: Are there any restrictions on diet?**

A: No but most are vegetarians. This may contradict no killing, but those meat eaters claim that if they did not kill then it is OK to eat meat.

102. **Q: Do they fast?**

A: Sometimes some do on those Holy days.

103. **Q: Are there any restrictions on dress?**

A: This depends on which group one belongs to e.g. Zen Monks wear black or brown rectangular robes of different colours of robes.

Theravada Bhikkhu wear brownish-yellow robes, Nuns wear brown or white and postulants of both male and female wear white.

Dharmacharis and Dhamacharinis of the Triratana Buddhists wear embroidered white Kesari.

104. **Q: What is Lama?**

A: A teacher in Tibetan tradition.

105. **Q: How do they deal with their deaths?**

A: Dead bodies are exposed to vultures, cremation or burial and the skeleton may be donated to a monastery for mediation purposes.

106. **Q: How is their marriage performed?**

A: A civil contract as per country protocols.

107. **Q: Are there any specific sacred writings?**

A: No, there are many.

108. **Q: What are the five main things/conducts that every Buddhist is to abide by?**

A:

1. Not to kill
2. Must be generous, not to steal
3. Stick to your partner and no sexual misconduct
4. Avoid lies, deceit or four-letter words
5. Do not drink alcohol.

109. **Q: What are the four philosophies?**

A:

1. The Karma can suffer.
2. On non-satisfaction known as dukkha.
3. Craving (tanha) cause suffering and make one valueless
4. Free yourself from grandiose or unworthy delusions (Samsara leads to nirvana).

The Four Noble truths leads one to Enlightenment.

110. **Q: What are the 8 noble truths?**

A: 1. Right understanding

2. Right speech

3. Right occupation

4. Right awareness

5. Right attitude

6. Right action

7. Right affront

8. Right composure.

111. **Q: How do Buddhists achieve these?**

A: They achieve these by discipline through meditation, Yoga and concentrating on good thoughts, giving to charity, sacrificing and spending time in the sacred temple.

112. **Q: Name the two forms of Buddhism in India.**

A: In the third century King Asoka supported the Buddhist doctrine (Theravada) he, his son and daughter spread it to Sri Lanka, Thailand, Burma. Theravada is/was very close to Buddha's teachings.

The second one is Mahayana Buddhism, which means Greater Vehicle.

113. **Q: What is the main difference between the two?**

A: Although it contains some of the original, its main philosophy includes: to achieve a goal – nirvana – one must consider others not just him/herself, so that one can gain satisfaction in (Puja) or worship and devotion (bhakti).

114. **Q: What is the name Buddhism in China and Japan?**

A: Zen Buddhism. They used mediation C'han or za-zeh.

115. **Q: What is Tibetan Buddhism?**

A: This is regarded as Bodhisattva/Avalokiteshvara. It shows compassion and patriotism.

116. **Q: What is Bodhisattva?**

A: This is the doctrine agreement between the Theravada and Mahayana whereby the earliest doctrine of self-examination alone now combined with the later doctrine to consider for fellow humans as well (not just selfish but other people). This is agreed and known as

Bodhisattva popularly known as "Buddha-in-waiting". This resulted in both inward and outward practice, mediation and yoga.

117. **Q: What is Avalokiteshvara?**

A: It is Bodhisattva status with four hands holding a lotus, it is warmth and compassion.

118. **Q: What is mantra?**

A: This is a phrase or statement, or a short prayer repeated. For example, Roman Catholics repeat the Hail Mary repeatedly with the Lord's prayer said one at the start and one at the end. An example of Buddhism is "Om mani padme hum" or mani pad me means Jewel in the lotus or om and hum.

119. **Q: What is the advantage of a mantra?**

A: It helps concentration or meditation to focus on God.

120. **Q: What is mandala?**

A: It is an interactional relationship and known as meditation circle.

121. **Q: Where do you find Vajrayana?**

A: Vajrayana is Buddhism in India, Nepal, Tibet, China and Japan.

122. **Q: Do Buddhists worship Buddha?**

A: They do not worship him but there are different Buddhists.

123. **Q: I understand from Buddhist practice book that they kneel down in front of Buddha's image.**

A: I have read that book by Bhikkhu Khantipalo. Yes, they kneel down in front of Buddha's image and make an offering. But this is to show respect.

124. **Q: How do Buddhists view Buddha?**

A: Some regard him as the highest teacher in the world who received the Enlightenment, so they kneel or stand in front of him placing their hand on their forehead and then to the chest as they chant.

125. **Q: What is Anjali?**

A: Is an Asiatic language meaning a greeting by putting hands on the forehead or chest to confirm that they are for peace and have no weapons.

After the Anjali, they use the word *namo* (or homage). This is done by bending.

126. **Q: Whom do they prostrate to?**

A: To Buddha then to the content of the philosopher book *Dhamma* and then to Noble Sangha.

127. **Q: Who is Sangha?**

A: It is someone who has practiced well to Enlightenment and practice.

128. **Q: If Buddhists don't believe in God whom do they worship?**

A: They do not worship anybody, but they ask Buddha to help them achieve the enlightenment. Some Buddhists believe in God.

129. **Q: What are the qualities or refuges expected from Buddhism for Enlightenment?**

A: 1. Show compassion (Bhagavato) loving kindness. 2. Be pure of heart (Bhagavato Arahato). 3. Wisdom (Samma Sambuddhassa).

All Buddhists aims are to be perfect – Samma.

130. **Q: What is the name given to the final stage in Buddhism?**

A: "Enlightenment" or "to the awakened".

131. **Q: Who is a true Buddhist?**

A: Anyone who accepts and practices the qualities or refuge or (Tisarana): Buddha (person), Dhamma (the philosophy book) and Sangho (practice religiously).

132. **Q: Where can Buddha's views on precepts be found?**

A: It is believed that Buddha said the following, which is in the *Dhammapada* (vv 246–7) and was based on the Precepts.

133. **Q: Can you quote a Buddhist saying?**

A: From the Dhammapada:

"Whoever destroys living beings speaks false words, who in the world takes that which is not given to him or goes too with another wife, or takes distilled, fermented drinks. Whatever man indulges thus extirpates the roots of himself, even here in this very world."

134. **Q: What are the five precepts?**

A: They are also called (Pancasila in Asian language) and imbued as Buddha said above:

Do not kill living creatures, do not steal, do not have sex with somebody else's wife, avoid false lies and deceit, do not become intoxicated.

135. **Q: What did Buddha say in Dhp 27?**

A: Do not engage in heedlessness, do not come near to sexual joys. The heedful and contemplative, attains abundant bliss. Buddhists regard the full moon as most important.

136. **Q: What is the main teaching of Buddhism?**

A: Understanding that life involves pain and suffering. Buddhism's promised route out of both suffering and the round of birth, death and rebirth.

137. **Q: Which countries are most populated by Buddhism?**

A: Now it is the whole world, but it first spread to East and Southwards to China, Japan, Southeast Asia.

138. **Q: What is the approximate population?**

A: Over 376 million.

139. **Q: How was Buddha physically described in the Pali?**

A: Buddha was described to have blue hair and golden skin (canon is a collective name for Buddhism teaching).

140. **Q: How did Buddha die?**

A: He ate some poisoned food (unknowingly). As he became aware of imminent death, he told his followers not to eat that food, he then lay down, meditated and died.

141. **Q: Was Buddha considered as God?**

A: No.

142. **Q: What are the five moral precepts (Pancha Sila) which all Buddhists are encouraged to live?**

A:

1. Not to harm living things (hence most are vegetarian) and avoid sports that result in blood.

2. Not to take what does not belong to you, i.e. no stealing, no begging (but can accept charitable gifts).

3. No misconduct involving the senses (no sexual misconduct).

4. Abstain from false speech – no lying, gossiping or offensive remarks.
5. Not to consume intoxicating substances (drugs or alcohol) and to make proper moral choices.

Chapter 3

Christianity

143. **Q: Who is the Lord?**

A: With capital "L" refers to Lord Jesus but the confusion is in the UK; they use capital L for with wisdom (earthly) or experience in his job, e.g. House of Lords.

144. **Q: Why did the disciples use "L" Lord?**

A: The original meaning is "master" for Jesus but Lord was and is used for the rich or ruler or men of God by their subordinates.

145. **Q: How do people express loss of hope in God?**

A: My faith is dwindling; my sin has engulfed my faith, there is no point of worshipping God, I am lapsed monotheists, faith is low.

146. **Q: Who controls the heart and mind?**

A: The creator but He gave freedom to humans to control them.

147. **Q: What makes people lose faith fully or partially?**

A:

a. When God appears not to answer supplication, facing hard times, this lead someone to sin or break the law of both God and country, their mind wanders during worship of God, become lazy to pray, do not abide by the posture recommended by the faith.

b. Some mental illnesses, such as reactive depression or anxiety, seclusion, moody, paranoia.

   Fight for leadership position without qualification.

c. Evangelic/preaching as a job hence they do not practice it.

d. One who is pleased for somebody's failure.

e. Show no remorse and feel it is not necessary to do good.

f. Break from the congregation.

g. One loses motivation to follow the Ten Commandments.

h. Phobia, i.e. fear of the unknown.

i. Panic when struck with illness.

j. Disputes leading to war, arguments, disrespect.

k. Word or earthly wealth takes over one's life.

l. Defence mechanism, exaggerating what one does not like.

m. When the above happens, the person may attempt to find what caused the lowering in faith:

n. Not going to God's house: church, temple, mosque, synagogue.

o. Show disinterest from faith.

p. Careless to read religious books.

q. Mixing with unbelievers.

r. More interest with the earthly riches including properties, friendship.

s. Sadness, unaware.

t. Worry about the future.

u.   Overindulgence with sleep, eating, parties, in undesirable company.

v.   Overcoming the lost or dwindling of hope.

w.   One needs to reflect and find what went wrong for them to lapse in faith.

x.   Start reading the books of God: Gita, Bible, Quran.

y.   Follow the Ten Commandments. Pray to your creator for guidance.

z.   Discuss about God in the company of the faith you belong.

aa. Love your neighbour which includes respect, honour and passion.

bb. Go on a pilgrimage.

cc. Fasting and praying to God/Allah/Sammy for help, repent and sow seeds.

dd. Charity work.

ee. Remind yourself that you will one day die and who can care for your soul and will you go to Heaven or Hell will depend what one sows on earth.

ff.   Think of the universe, not just the earth and consider who created the universe and everything within it. You will then appreciate God/Allah/Sammy.

gg.   It is good to think long-term but limit it to the middle term.

hh.   Associate with believers of the creator, it does not matter what faith the person belongs to.

ii.   Protect your life, be meek and loyal.

148.   **Q: How many stations are there of the cross?**

149.   **Q: Who pronounced at the trial that Jesus was   innocent?**

A:

a.   Judas Iscariot said, "I have sinned because I have betrayed an innocent man." He then committed suicide.

b.   Pilate said, "I am innocent of this just man's blood."

c.   The Centurion who saw Jesus crucified said, "Jesus was indeed a just man."

d.   Many people saw him pierced.

150. **Q: Why was Jesus humiliated?**

A: Human sin cost Jesus his life and humiliation.

151. **Q: Who helped him with the cross and why?**

A: Simon as an indication that humans will have to share his suffering and humiliation.

152. **Q: Why did Jesus allow the devoted religious woman to carry off an impression of Jesus as sacred countenance?**

A: Jesus allowed this to last to the future and to remind all humans of his image impressed on all human hearts.

153. **Q: How was Jesus crucified?**

A: Each hand was nailed to the cross and each foot too, his eyes were swollen and closed, his mouth was filled with vinegar and gall, his head was encircled by the sharp thorny crown, his sense mortified.

154. **Q: List briefly what happened at the station of the cross.**

A:

a. This was celebrating yearly by the Roman Catholic and a few churches.

b. 1st station = Jesus was condemned to death.

c. 2nd station = Jesus received his cross.

d. 3rd station = Jesus fell under the weight of the cross the first time.

e. 4th station = Jesus met his mother.

f. 5th station = Simon of Cyrene helped Jesus carry the cross.

g. 6th station = Jesus's face was wiped by Veronica.

h. 7th station = Jesus fell for the second time.

i. 8th station = the women of Jerusalem mourned for Jesus.

j. 9th station = Jesus fell for the third time.

k. 10th station = Jesus was stripped of his garments.

l. 11th station = Jesus was nailed to the cross.

m. 12th station = Jesus died upon the cross.

n. 13th station = Jesus was laid in the arms of his mother.

o. 14th station = Jesus was laid in the sepulchre.

155. **Q: What are the undisputed facts about Jesus Christ?**

A: He was borne by virgin Mary, that he was special, a messiah, performed many miracles. He was lifted to Heaven.

156. **Q: Name some of the branches of Christianity.**

A:

a. There are two groups of Christianity namely Episcopalians (accept the priest and bishops ordain). For example, Roman Catholics, Eastern Orthodox, Lutheran and Anglican Communion.

b. Non-Episcopalians include: Methodist, Reformed Baptists, Church of Scotland, Congregationalists, Pentecostal.

157. **Q: How is the Christian year divided?**

A:

a. Advent: preparation for Christmas

b. Christmas: preparation for Christmas

c. Lent: four days fasting to prepare for Easter

d. Palm Sunday: First day of Holy week

e. Good Friday: Jesus's death on the cross

f. Easter Sunday: Celebration of resurrection

g. Ascension Day: Jesus went back to Heaven

h. Pentecost/Whitsun: Day when Jesus sent Holy Spirit

i. Trinity Sunday: First Sunday after Pentecost.

158. **Q: Name a few Christian churches.**

A: Orthodox Church, Roman Catholic, Anglican, Protestantism.

159. **Q: Name a few Protestantism's.**

A: The Lutheran Church, Reform Church, Free Churches include Baptist, Methodist, Society of Friends, Salvation Army.

160. **Q: When and who formed some of these Protestantism's?**

A: The Baptists in 16 thcenturies by John Smyth, Methodists by John Wesley (1703–91), Society of Friends Quakers by George Fox (1624–91) and The Salvation Army by William Booth (1829–1912).

161. **Q: Are there some fringe movements?**

A:

a. Jehovah's Witnesses in nineteenth century by Charles Taze Russell.

b.   The Church of Christ Scientist in 1892 by Mary Baker Eddy.

c.   The Church of Jesus Christ (fringe movement) of Latter-Day Saints (Mormons) by Joseph Smith in 1827.

d.   Unification Church, 1954 by Reverend Sun Myung Moon.

e.   Unitarian Church in seventeenth century by John Biddle 1615–92.

162.   **Q: Name one Christian Church in China.**

A: Nestorian 1284.

163.   **Q: Name one Christian Church in India, Asia, Africa, South and North America.**

A:

a.   In India by St. Thomas the Apostle in the fourth century.

b.   In Asia – Roman Catholic in sixteenth century and Protestant.

c.   In Africa – Coptic Church nineteenth century (Egypt and Ethiopia).

d. North and South America – Calvinist Protestant, nineteenth century Roman Catholic, Orthodoxy.

e. Anglican Church by Archbishop Thomas Cranmer in 1549 by instruction of King Henry VIII in 1534.

164. **Q: At what age did Jesus begin teaching and how long?**

A: Jesus started teaching at 30 years for three years.

165. **Q: What message did Jesus bring to all humans?**

A: That God loves all humans unconditionally, to repent and to be born again.

166. **Q: How did Jesus sum up all the commandments?**

A: Jesus said *love your neighbour as yourself.*

167. **Q: What did Jesus' death do for humans?**

A: His death offered forgiveness and eternal life to the whole human race.

168. **Q: What is the significance of the last supper?**

A: It is a sacred act of worship. The communion in the name of the Father (God), Son (Jesus Christ) and Holy Spirit.

169. **Q: What happens in most Christian churches?**

A:

a. It consists of hymns, reading from the Bible, preaching, teaching and prayers. Sunday is the day of most Christian worship.

b. However, other Christian denominations have different days, for example Seven Day Adventist worship on Saturday.

c. Roman Catholics do have communion mass Monday to Friday in addition to Sunday.

d. Saturday is usually for confession of sin to the priest/father who represent Jesus Christ.

170. **Q: What are the Holy days for Christmas?**

A:

a. Christmas Day (25 thDecember)

b. Ash Wednesday (after Jesus 40 days fasting) and being tempted by Satan.

c. Maundy Thursday to celebrate the last supper or Eucharist.

d. Good Friday: death of Jesus.

e. Easter Sunday: Resurrection of Jesus.

f. Ascension Day: Date Jesus ascended to Heaven.

g. Pentecost: When the Holy Spirit descended on the disciples.

171. **Q: When do Christians fast?**

A: Lent to remember Jesus's 40 days of fasting. Lent is Roman Catholics ritual recommended to members to fast for a few hours and to give up something they like.

There is no special rule of when people should fast and the ritual behind it.

172. **Q: Are there any initiation or Rites in Christianity?**

A: Baptism: To welcome a child or adult into Christianity. Using water as symbols of cleansing away the sin.

173. **Q: Confirmation: When the person is older it affirms his/her faith in Christianity.**

A:

a. Laying on the hands/anointing oil: Healing with prayers and miracles.

b. Marriage: This binds man and woman together.

c. Death/Dying: Usually a Christian priest offers last office.

174. **Q: How do you prove God's existence?**

A: By the existence of the Universe, solar system and answering our prayers (James Safo's personal experience).

175. **Q: Does God speak to people?**

A: Yes. In the Toran (five books – 500 times) and almost 4,000 times in the Old Testament.

176. **Q: Who and what does God like?**

A: He is the alpha and omega (first and last). He is a spirit, has no physical characteristics, he is eternal, independent, Holy, just, perfect.

177. **Q: Where does sin come from?**

A: Adam and Eve's sin by disobeying God in the Garden of Eden.

178. **Q: What is sin?**

A: Any human behaviour which is not in accordance with God. Sin is lawlessness, defiance, defilement, debasement.

179. **Q: What will happen on the day of judgement?**

A: God will judge us (human beings) and the final punishment will be delivered.

180. **Q: What is Hell like?**

A: Hell is factual, fearful and final (4 x F) and fair (since God will judge everyone with justness).

181. **Q: If we have religion can we satisfy God?**

A: Yes, if you have 100% faith, trust and believe in God. But religion alone never satisfies God. It cannot wipe out our sin or sinful nature.

182. **Q: Why did Jesus come to earth and to die?**

A: To wipe out our sin, hence he was a sin-bearer, he was the saviour. His death on the cross is the undisputed belief of all Christians.

I must say that the Muslims did not believe that the real Jesus was crucified on the cross Christians. Some feel that God would not allow human beings to humiliate his special messenger especially "only begotten son" as Christians believe.

183. **Q: How can God save us?**

A: First repent your sin, then have faith and trust in God, pray, read the Holy books: Bible, fellowship; go to church.

184. **Q: Is there any dispute from the major faith and the content of the Tora (first five books of the Old Testament) and why?**

A: No. It is believed that it was God himself who delivered the content to mankind through Moses. The rest of the Old Testament is also respected as God's servants received instructions from God. The temptation, life of some of the servants, e.g. Jog, Esther, Jonah are testament to humans to follow of God's being the creator, overseer, geometrician, alpha and omega, etc. of the universe.

185. **Q: Name some of the major prophets in the Old Testament.**

A: Isaiah, Jeremiah, Ezekiel, Daniel, Elijah, Elisha.

186. **Q: Name some of the minor prophets of the Old Testament.**

A: Hosea, Joel, Amos, Obadiah, Jonah, Micah, Nahum, Habakkuk, Zephaniah, Haggai, Malachi, Zephaniah.

187. **Q: Which part of the Old Testament is the prophetic history?**

A: Joshua, Judges, 1 Samuel, 2 Samuel, 1 Kings, 2 Kings.

188. **Q: Which are the historic books?**

A: 1 Chronicles, 2 Chronicles, Ezra, Nehemiah, 1 Maccabees, 2 Maccabees.

189. **Q: Which ones are the writings?**

A: Job, Proverbs, Ecclesiastes, Song of Songs, Ruth, Lamentation, Esther, Judith, Baruch, Psalms, New Testament.

190. **Q: Who are the Four Gospels?**

A: Matthew, Mark, Luke and John.

191. **Q: In the New Testament, it is believed that St. Paul wrote letters to who?**

A: Romans, 1 Corinthians, 2 Corinthians, Galatians, Ephesians, Philippians, Colossians,

Philemon, 1 Thessalonians, 2 Thessalonians, 1 Timothy, 2 Timothy, Titus, Hebrews.

192. **Q: Who are referred to as Epistles?**

A: James, 1 Peter, 2 Peter, 1 John, 2 John, 3 John, Jude, Revelation.

193. **Q: In the Old Testament, who were the two great powers during Abraham about 2000–1750?**

A: Egypt and Mesopotamia.

194. **Q: Why do some people pray to the Saints, e.g. prayer to St. Joseph by Divine Mercy, publication in Dublin.**

A: It would be ok to ask righteous people, e.g. saints, prophets or Jesus to intercede for you. Even Jesus said pray to God or ask him to pray for you. Prophets or saints never gave any form of intension for anyone to pray to them for their needs.

Christian Science Church

195. **Q: Who and when was Christian science founded?**

A: Mary Baker Eddy founded science and health in 1879.

196. **Q: How did Christian science come into being?**

A: Mary Baker Eddy was miraculously healed after a very serious accident and when she was reading one of Jesus' healings, she herself was healed.

197. **Q: What are their principles or beliefs?**

A: The spiritual healing is the outcome of prayers and spiritual renewal. They believe that God heals physically, psychologically and forgives sins.

198. **Q: What Holy book do they use?**

A: King James' version of the Bible.

199. **Q: Where is the mother church?**

A: Church of Christ, scientist, in Boston, USA.

200. **Q: Are there any restrictions?**

A: No restrictions on diet, dress, funerals, weddings.

201. **Q: What is the title page of scriptures book?**

A: *The Book of Mormons Jesus is the Christ, the Eternal God* encourages Christian science to learn from the Bible that Jesus Christ was the Son of God who came to earth to overcome sins.

202. **Q: How do they worship and dress?**

A: There are no restrictions on dress, they worship on Sundays consisting of singing, praying, lessons and spiritual reading.

203. **Q: Are there any food restrictions?**

A: No, save normal tea and coffee is forbidden.

204. **Q: Do they fast?**

A: Yes, one day a month.

205. **Q: Are there any festivals?**

A: Yes, Christmas.

206. **Q: How does one get advice?**

A: Please visit Mormon.org and ids.org.

207. **Q: Who and when was the Methodist Church?**

A: John Wesley and his brother Charles Wesley.

208. **Q: Why did they form the church?**

A: They defected from the Church of England and believe in the Moravian Church.

209. **Q: So why didn't he stay in the Church of England?**

A: In 1738 John Wesley said, "I felt I did trust Christ, in Christ alone for my salvation and an assurance was given me that Christ has taken away mine sin, even mine and saved me from the law of sin and death."

210. **Q: What about the Church of England?**

A: King James left the Catholic Church because he was now allowed to divorce and marry again.

211. **Q: Is this not abuse of power over so many people?**

A: The congregation were not forced, they had their choice.

212. **Q: Who founded the Salvation Army?**

A: It was formed by William Booth in 1861.

213. **Q: What about the Presbyterians?**

A: They worship God and they believe every person pre-ordains destiny.

Quakers

214. **Q: Who founded the Quakers?**

A: Mr George Fox founded it around 1652. Quaker members are all friends. It is a religious society.

215. **Q: Whom do they worship?**

A:

a. They worship God in silence, no formal, no priest. Non-violent, no communion.

b. They are looking for the truth.

Baptist Church

216. **Q: What about the Baptist Church?**

A: It was formed by a group from Holland and England.

217. **Q: Where are they dominant?**

A: USA, congregation, independent, appoint Deacons.

218. **Q: What is their conviction?**

A: They are democratic and have a missionary.

Pentecostals Church

219. **Q: Why do you think the Pentecostals waited for nearly 2000 years after the Holy Spirit allegedly came on the followers of Christ to form this?**

80

A: I am told that the Christian churches, by marketing and domineering, did brainwash a lot of people before they were awakened.

220. **Q: Don't you think the fact that it started in America was just business to make a few people rich?**

A: I understand they wished to come out from a more rigid formal worship of God.

221. **Q: Their movement is like partly lively where they go to enjoy themselves not God.**

A: The Bible, especially some of the Psalms, for example Psalm 150, and many said clearly to praise and worship God with their trumpets, harps, tambourines and dancing, stringed instruments, woodwinds, cymbals. Psalm 148 said shout the Lord Praises; Psalm 149 said Praise God by dancing, play music on harps, songs on your lips.

222. **Q: Why do only the Pentecostal praise God in this way?**

A: Everybody has ways of expressing their worship and glorifying God, as Psalm 148:11 that one can praise God's name.

223. **Q: Who else praises or worships your God?**

A: The living things, including humans, must worship and praise God, including the sun, moon, stars, Heaven, water, fire, monsters, mountains and hills, trees, hail, snow, frost, wind, Kings, Queens, etc.

224. **Q: The way they shout, behave, throwing themselves upon the floor, speaking and believing... Don't you think they are odd?**

A: I don't think so. It is their way of expressing things.

225. **Q: James, be real, mentally and physiologically... They appear to behave like the devil possesses them, hearing voices, seeing and imagining things, i.e. hallucinating visually and auditorily.**

A: Trust you to say things that hurt. I hope they do not take you seriously, because they believe to cast your followers devil out of humans just as Jesus Christ did.

226. **Q: Speak in tongues ... they do not understand.**

A: Like every movement/organisation, you may get people who may behave evilly like you.

227. **Q: Why did they ask congregations to pay more than one contribution?**

A: Policies differ from one organisation to another.

228. **Q: Why is it that the Holy Spirit comes upon Pentecostal members and makes them speak in a different tone?**

A: I hope you show some respect.

229. **Q: So how many members are there?**

A: It is very fast growing and spreading all over the world of over 100 million people.

230. **Q: People who throw themselves upon the floor show signs and symptoms of grand mal or major epileptic fits.**

A: Satan, you are pathetic, and I think we must end this dialogue. There are many explanations for them to fall.

231. **Q: Name some reasons why fall and have convulsion symptoms?**

A: I am told that sometimes the holy spirit manifests itself in that manner.

Also, when the person is possessing by evil spirit and during deliverance the person have no control of his or her action.

Or if the person is anointed with oil by the priest/prophet.

232. **Q: Why is it that this occurs mainly among black Africans especially about 95% of these are women?**

A: I am afraid I have not been given any positive reasons for this, but I have been told that there are more evil spirits and witches or witchcraft? among black Africans.

233. **Q: How could there be evil spirits when Christians believe in God?**

A: You Satan are the leader of the evil spirit. In the Holy Bible, it confirms that there are evil spirits and in fact Jesus cast out such spirits from a woman possessed.

234. **Q: Why is every Christian not allowed to receive the body and blood of Christ in any church?**

A: In theory, I agree but every organisation such as churches, Freemasonry, etc. have rituals and conditions to receive communion.

235. **Q: Why is the Queen the head of the Church of England?**

A: The Queen inherited from the founder King Henry and it has always been passed on within the Royal family.

But the day-to-day religious decisions are taken by the archbishop.

236. **Q: In recent years some Pentecostal churches led by a self-ordained prophet or Pistol do ask the congregation to pay a specific amount such as one thousand pounds or five hundred pounds during the**

offering. **Sometimes this is under the pretence for the prophecy to come true.**

A: I personally will not attend such an organisation, but peoples' belief, and exercising of their free will must be respected.

237. **Q: What about pastors who demand these in the name of Jesus?**

A: There is nothing in the Bible of Jesus or his disapplies demanding money for miracles performed.

The church has expenses, but congregations must give freely what they can afford.

238. **Q: Why is it that the powerful religious leaders such as the Pope of Roman Catholic and the Queen of Church of England or Anglican church does not use their powers to prevent wars or aggression?**

A: Wars are political decisions. Jesus said give unto Caesar what for Caesar and unto God what Gods.

239. **Q: Why does God not swiftly revenge on wicked people as per Psalm 91 and 92?**

A: God time of revenge is the best. Remember that God created the wicked people and liked to give them time to repent.

Rastafari

240. **Q: Who formed Rastafarianism?**

A: Marcus Garvey.

241. **Q: When, who and where was Rastafari founded?**

A: Rastafari was founded in 1930 in Jamaica. It was believed to have been by "Rastafari" who was known as Haile Selassie I, Emperor of Ethiopia.

242. **Q: What is their main belief?**

A:

a. That an African king would be the Messiah.

b. That all blacks to go back to Africa, non-violence, belief in divinity of Emperor Hail Selassie and condemnation of Babylon who took Jews as slaves.

243. **Q: Who do they link themselves with?**

A: Rastafarians combine their belief and interests in Christians and African-Caribbean nations.

244. **Q: What is their first belief?**

A: They believe that they are God's chosen people, not the Israelites.

245. **Q: Why do Rastafarians believe in their hair style?**

A: In the Bible Leviticus 21:5 "They shall not make baldness upon their heads, neither shall they shave off the corner of their beards nor make any cuttings in their flesh."

246. **Q: How would you notice them?**

A: Dreadlock hair and wearing of their flag red, gold and green.

247. **Q: Where in the Holy book does it support their religion?**

A: Genesis 3:18 "Thorns also and thistles shall it bring forth to you and you shall eat the herb of the field." They support this because God said it to Adam.

248. **Q: These people smoke illegal drugs.**

A: It may be illegal in some countries but the Rastafarians claim to smoke it for certain reasons.

249. **Q: What for, to hallucinate or to be deluded?**

A: Could you please show respect for equality and discrimination.

250. **Q: So why do they smoke?**

A: Some do it for religious reasons, which they call it the gange or "wisdom weed" or holy weed.

251. **Q: How many are there at present in the world?**

A: Possibly less than one million.

252. **Q: You know I am not going to comment on that. No please, do not dodge answering my question.**

A: Ras Tafari Makonnen was an orthodox Christian, so are most of his subjects in Ethiopia.

253. **Q: What are their main rituals?**

A: Reasoning, which is an informal meeting and SMOK ganga and binghi – held on special occasions, including Hails Salissi coronation on 2nd November and his birthday 6th January.

254. **Q: What is another name for ganga and its significance?**

A: Marijuana. Ganga is regarded as "wisdom weed", which aids mediation.

255. **Q: Is there any proof that God allows ganga?**

A: Yes Genesis 3:18 "Thou shalt eat the herb of the field."

256. **Q: What are the main sects in Rastafarian?**

A: Bobos and the 12 tribes of Israel.

257. **Q: Which of the two groups did Bob Marley belong to?**

A: The Twelve Tribes of Israel.

258. **Q: What is the name Rastafarian given to God?**

A: Jah.

259. **Q: What is or are their Holy books?**

A: There are three, namely the Bible, Kebra Negast and Fetha Negast.

260. **Q: What is the view of most Rastafarians?**

A: They have firm beliefs that their roots are from African ancestors. They dislike the white culture who were forced to be slaves?

261. **Q: Where do they regard as the Promised Land?**

A: Ethiopia.

262. **Q: How do they support this?**

A: Some of them believe that Ethiopia is an empire (it has never been ruled by any country) and that three popes originated from Egypt and Ethiopia and that it was the centre of God's choice.

263. **Q: Why did they come to believe that they were God's chosen people and that Ethiopia is the Promised Land?**

A: Their view is supported by the Bible. Kings Chapter 10, verse 4 and 5 expanded in other Holy books of Rastafari, Kebra, Negast (Glory to God).

264. **Q: What religious name do they associate Haile Selassie?**

A:

a. They called him Lord Ras Tafari being head of Creator, conquered Judah, Haile Selassie, Power of the Trinity, King of Kings, Lord of

Lords. They believe in the marriage of King Solomon and the Queen of Sheba.

b. I couldn't see in most Bibles the connection of this as Ethiopia's name was not mentioned in both 1st or 2 nd King 10:4–5 and 13.

265. **Q: How does the Bible support Rastafari and the true Messiah (not Jesus) and the promised homeland being Ethiopia?**

A: They support this by quoting the Bible Genesis 2:13. Research revealed that one of the five rivers from Eden Gihon passes through Ethiopia. I cannot trace any concrete proof in the Bible.

266. **Q: Why do the Rastafarians smoke marijuana?**

A: They believe that marijuana gives them mystical experiences used in worship.

267. **Q: Name one concept of Rastafari.**

A: The most used mission statement or motto is "Peace and Love, Justice for all".

268. **Q: Which of the two groups did Bob Marley belong to?**

A: The Twelve Tribes of Israel.

269. **Q: Why do Rastafarians believe in their hair style?**

A: In the Bible Leviticus 21:5 "They shall not make baldness upon their heads, neither shall they shave off the corner of their beards nor make any cuttings in their flesh."

270. **Q: What other symbols are prominent in Rastafarianism?**

A: They sometimes wear the colour of religion as their belief: red, gold and green stands for the blood of martyrs, wealth and beauty or vegetation.

271. **Q: Was Emperor Haile Selassie a Rastafarian?**

A: This is one of your sensible questions.

272. **Q: Hi, James. Are you saying I ask silly? questions?**

A: Yes, I am afraid so, because religious intolerance of some of your stupid questions. I think you do that to get people upset or tempt them.

273. **Q: You know I am not going to comment on that. No please, do not dodge answering my question.**

A: An orthodox: Ras Tafari Makonnen was a Christian, so are most of his subjects in Ethiopia.

274. **Q: Why do they worship him?**

A: I think because he was the first leader of the country, which is an Empire to accept and respect them.

275. **Q: But he did not show any characteristics.**

A: He did not have dreadlock hair and never smoked ganga. But he made a state visit to Jamaica and was well welcomed by over 90% Rastafarians. He spent time visiting them. It was believed that miracles occurred

276. **Q: How were Angels and Jinn created?**

A: Angels were created from light and Jinn spirits created from fire.

277. **Q: What is the difference between humans and Angels?**

A: Angels were given knowledge and act as messengers between God the father, Jesus Christ the son and humans.

278. **Q: What about the Holy Spirit and Angels?**

A: Christians believe that the Holy Spirit are within us and humans need to develop it. They also believe Angels are always around us.

Muslims do not believe in the Holy Spirit but believe that each human has at least one angel always.

279. **Q: Why are humans now higher than Angels?**

A: Humans are higher than Angels because God has given humans the power to develop their knowledge, wisdom, creative thought, speech, invention, overcoming things, etc.

280. **Q: What is the angels' attitude?**

A: Angels feel this superiority will make man's ability to do more harm than good to the earth, environment and to each other, e.g. war etc.

Nevertheless, Angels readily accept, submit and bow to first man Adam.

281. **Q: How does God overcome his anger, wrath?**

A: God is full of mercy, he overcomes his anger. He is quick to forgive and slow to anger.

282. **Q: How would you interpret human occupation on earth?**

A: Humans are renting or their occupation on earth is temporary; where humans have been given the choice to express their intentions or trials and test whether they obey the way of life as laid down in the Ten Commandments, which are in the Holy books, i.e. Bible and Quran and other philosophy books.

283. **Q: How does God's spirit relate to humans?**

A: If humans follow the guidance (way of life) and commandments it will help humans to fulfil their true potential of living up to the spirit of God in them as his representative on earth or to follow the devil into obeying their base desires, which will eventually betray their humble material makeup.

284. **Q: What is Faith tradition?**

A: Christians, Judaism, Islamists, Hindus, Sikhs, etc. summarise that the fear of God is the crown of all knowledge.

285. **Q: How does God help humans to remember that he is the Lord, Creator of the Universe?**

A: He sent his messengers, Angels and his own son to emphasise his guidance.

286. **Q: Why do the Islamists call God Allah?**

A: Christians use capital letter "G" for God and use small letter "g" for gods or idol. Allah is unique. He has no equal and He (Allah) shares his name none else. There is no other Allah but him. It demonstrates Islam's total commitment to Allah all knowing, all seeing.

287. **Q: How do we trace the name Allah?**

A: Allah can be found in the old scriptures in the cousin language of Arabi, Hebrew and Aramaic. In the Bible, we can find *Eli* which stands for Allah (Jesus called Eli, Eli, Samathana– my God my God why have thou forsaken me). In the Bible the name Elohim stands for "Allahumm" or "O Allah".

288. **Q: Why do all faiths have different names for God/Allah?**

A: God/Allah/Nan name have so many attributes for different faiths, they are used to confirm positive respect and love for Him. All the attributes have beautiful names to describe the Creator of the universe and everything within.

Some of these are exclusive to him alone exclusively and others describe his qualities or attributes, e.g. All seeing, all knowing, All merciful. He is just generous.

Islamists have ninety-nine names for Allah. They guarantee for any Islamist using Allah's name to enter paradise is to remember and apply the knowledge to have Allah/God in individuals' lives will be filled with virtue and crowned with rewards.

Whilst Buddhists have Enlightenment as the ultimate truth, in Muslims Allah is the ultimate truth.

289. **Q: Jesus initially said he was God's slave. What is the Islamists version?**

A: To Muslim/Islam it is an honour to be a devoted slave of Allah because that individual's master is the Creator, overseer, geometrician of the universe. Every believer strives to be accepted as God's/Allah's slave. It gives strength, courage and dignity to the individual.

290. **Q: How does God get his words to people?**

A: Messengers, Prophets, spirit, Angels, son of God. These prophets chosen by God must have good character and be impeccable who can bring the message of God and set a personal example. God gives these messengers insight so that they can prophesise or predict the future. It depends on what degree of gift is given to the messenger.

291. **Q: Name some insights given to prophets?**

A: David and Prophet Muhammad were given the gift of revelation of the Psalms and Quran. Jesus Christ was given the gift of wisdom, knowledge, healing, miracles, etc. Before he came, no other prophet was given the authority to perform what he did.

Jesus also warned us about false prophets.

292. **Q: Does the priest, Rabbi, Imran, Fathers, Sisters practice what they preach?**

A: Some church leaders are not prophets so one should listen to the interpretation of the scriptures without following their example. They have the knowledge.

293. **Q: How did God choose a prophet?**

A: God always chose a prophet from among their own people, who speak their own language. most of prophet work was attributed to all of mankind.

All God's prophets came out with the same doctrine of God.

294. **Q: Which messenger can you see both in the Quran and the Bible?**

A: Adam (Idris), Noah (Nuh), Hud, Salih, Lot (Lut), Abraham (Ibrahim), Ishmael (Ism'il), Isaac (Ishaq), Jacob (Ya qub), Joseph (Yusuf), Jethro (Shu'ayb), Job (Ayyub), Moses (Musa), Aaron (Harun), David (Dawud), Solomon (Sulayman), Jonah (Yunus), Elijah (Ilyas), Elisha (Al-Yasa),

Zakariyya (Dhul-kifi), John (Yahja), Jesus (Isa), Muhammad.

295. **Q: What makes Islamists special?**

A: The answer I got was that the Islamists look ahead, i.e. life after death is certainly not a possibility. The Islamists believe human existence is temporary.

Before Jesus Christ came to the earth God communicated directly to humans. Let us try to see who God was speaking to.

296. **Q: What did God order the angels when Adam was created and put in the paradise garden?**

A: Bow down to Adam.

297. **Q: What was the warning God gave to Adam in the paradise garden?**

A: You must never eat the fruit from this tree (tree of knowledge of good and evil). If you disobey me I will punish you.

298. **Q: Why have you covered yourselves with leaves? Why are you ashamed of your nakedness? now when you have always**

walked freely and unabashed? Take these furs and cover yourselves.

A: Adam and Eve.

299. **Q: What did God said to Adam and Eve after they had eaten the forbidden fruit?**

A: Have you eaten the fruit of knowledge from the forbidden tree?

300. **Q: I gave you everything, yet you disobeyed me.**

A: Adam and Eve.

301. **Q: What was the punishment to the snake?**

A: You will never live as you please again. You will never walk with men or with angels. You will slide on the ground on your belly and will eat the dust from the earth. Men will always despise you.

302. **Q: What punishment did God gave to man (Adam)?**

A: You have lost the benefit of the Paradise garden. You will toil and sweat from the rising of the sun to the rising of the moon…

303. **Q: What was the woman's punishment (Eve)?**

A: You will have pain and sweat during labour when you have children.

304. **Q: What other punishment was given to both man (Adam) and woman (Eve)?**

A: Both of you will return to dust, filled with fear and pain before you die.

305. **Q: Was Abraham a Christian or Islamist?**

A: Neither as the names or the leaders didn't exist at that time (Jesus and Muhammad).

306. **Q: Who did they worship?**

A: They worshipped God directly in any manner or posture they decided.

307. **Q: Did Abraham commit adultery by sleeping with Hagar (his wife's maid)?**

A: No. At that time men could practice polygamy. Abraham married Hagar before he made her pregnant.

308. **Q: How or what was special about Abraham?**

A: Sarah (Abraham's wife) proposed for Abraham to sleep with young Hagar since Sarah was barren and past child bearing age.

Also, God approved the marriage between Abraham and Hagar because God blessed Ismael who was Hagar and Abraham's son.

309. **Q: Don't you agree that Sarah and Abraham set president to us all – i.e. adultery?**

A: No. Abraham did not cheat on Sarah.

310. **Q: If the Islamists claimed Abraham was Islam, and if most of the men of Abraham practiced polygamy then Abraham was Islam?**

A: Islam became a religion after the revelation of the Quran over thousands of years after Abraham's death.

No. In a lot of countries Africa, Jamaica, Cuba the Christians do practice polygamy. It depends on the law of each country.

311. **Q: So, when God said do not commit adultery what did it mean?**

A: If your country law is to practice polygamy then you must marry the person before having sex with her which is what most Christians believe and try to impose on their children.

312. **Q: Who is the king of kings?**

A: The answer is God but since Jesus and his father are one the king of kings is Jesus.

313. **Q: Nearly 2000 years ago Jesus said the day of judgement will be soon. Jehovah witnesses predicted the year 2000, which has come and gone. So when will it be?**

A: Nobody knows the judgement day which only God the father knows. Just be prepared.

314. **Q: When did Jesus receive the Holy Spirit?**

A: This was at the age of 30 when he was being baptised by John the Baptist. The Heaven opened and said, "This is my beloved son whom I am well pleased. Listen to him."

315. **Q: What did Jesus have before the age of 30?**

A: He was born with the highest wisdom (more than Solomon).

316. **Q: How do we know this?**

A: At the age of 12 he was in the synagogue with the top priest, Rabbi and his contribution was above all their knowledge. They were amazed of his wisdom.

317. **Q: Did Jesus' earthly parents Joseph and Mary tell him about the angel Gabriel appearing to them?**

A: No, because God made them forget.

318. **Q: John the Baptist's parents Zechariah and Elizabeth were very old, how was John conceived?**

A: This is a hard one. We know that John's mother was not a virgin because they had been trying for a baby unsuccessfully. One will assume when they last made love that this was when John was conceived.

319. **Q: John and Jesus were cousins. Didn't they know their mission?**

A: Yes. It can be argued but their parents forgot or God wiped it from their knowledge.

320. **Q: When did they know?**

A: With John when he was in the wilderness and started baptising people and prophesised the coming of the Messiah (he did not know Jesus was the Messiah).

321. **Q: When did John know Jesus was the Messiah?**

A: He did not know until Jesus was standing in the crowd and then went to the water to be baptised, then he knew it because John told Jesus that He, Jesus, should baptise John. It was after the baptism that the Holy Spirit came upon Jesus like a dove.

322. **Q: Did Jesus's earthly brothers and sisters become one of the disciples?**

A: Mary had children and it was believed that James was one of the 12 disciples. This answer is refuted by the Roman Catholic faith who believe Mary died as a virgin.

323. **Q: When Jesus was building or selecting his 12 disciples, why was it that whoever he called just dropped everything and followed him?**

A: Since he chose 12 disciples before he started healings and miracles I would suspect that they were pre-ordained by God.

324. **Q: Which of the current faiths has the most problems?**

A: I would say the Christians because there are about 63,000 Christian denominations as evidence of division among them.

325. **Q: When God spoke and the Holy Spirit came to Jesus, who heard the words?**

A: I suspect Jesus and John heard it, then a few chosen among the crowd and there were people in the mountain who also heard it. That is when Jesus grew in confidence.

326. **Q: Was Jesus confused of who he was at the beginning?**

A: No. He was a humble man, hence he first claimed to be a slave of God, then Messenger, Prophet then after his baptism Son of God because he heard it.

327. **Q: Why did Jesus ask his disciples who he was?**

A: To test their knowledge and Peter said Son of God.

328. **Q: What do you mean by Jesus being humble?**

A: Yes, he was. He did not take credit for healing, miracles and wisdom, he asked God for permission and he made sure people were aware that God's permission was granted.

329. **Q: Why do Christians call Jesus God?**

A: Jesus never said he was God, he said he was the son of God his father. In fact, the prayers he thought Christians start as "Our father, who art in heaven…"

330. **Q: What does he mean that Father God and him are one?**

A: It means that Jesus and God have the same attributes and that both are alike.

331. **Q: Why did Jesus say Christians should ask God in his name and they will get what they ask for?**

A: After the resurrection, he had fulfilled God's request and He (Jesus) were given the authority of the earth and Heaven so whatever one asks God, using Jesus as the mediator is guaranteed or something better. This will be as per God's own perfect time.

332.   **Q: James, do not beat about the bush, why do some Christians call Jesus as God?**

A: Out of 63,000 Christian denominations, only Roman Catholics, Church of England, Methodists, Anglicans believe in the Trinity, i.e. God the Father, God the son and God the Holy Spirit.

The human body is a temple for the Holy Spirit and one needs to activate it.

333.   **Q: Some Christians believe that God himself came to earth as Jesus.**

A: No. The son came. Remember at the beginning God created humans in his own image.

334.   **Q: People in India believe that God came to the East as human.**

A: Nothing is impossible for God. India had a few Avatars and strong beliefs that Lord Krishna was God. The biggest book in the world is Lord Krishna.

335. **Q: Do Christians believe Jesus is God?**

A: Shut up, Satan. I have already explained this. The closet Jesus went about this topic is, "My Father and I are one. I in him and He in Me." Jesus said, "I will send the Holy Spirit to you."

336. **Q: What about Prophet Muhammad?**

A: Prophet Muhammad never claimed to be God. In fact, he claimed the Arch Angel Gabriel appealed to him over a period of 23 years.

337. **Q: Since Jesus went to Heaven why have both God and Jesus gone quiet?**

A: Almighty God, the son and Holy Spirit are in communication with humans every second, 24-hours, 365/366 days a year directing, healing, performing miracles, destroying, etc.

338. **Q: Why do natural disasters continue to make innocent people die?**

A: God has not changed. Since Jesus went back to Heaven God continued to punish people, exalt the righteous, speak through men of God.

339. **Q: You mean false prophets?**

A: Human beings are the best judge if the person who claims to be a prophet has the quality of God or false (Satan) prophet.

340. **Q: Can I repent last minute to go to Heaven, just as the criminal crucified with Jesus did?**

A: No. Not when you know what you did and decided to wait. In fact, you will not get the chance because Judgement Day will be unexpected and as soon as God or Jesus comes, that will be the end of repentance and the beginning of judgement (up to 30 minutes).

341. **Q: James, Mr Know-It-All, what do you suggest Satan and my followers do to go to Heaven?**

A: I do not claim to know it all and I resist your temptation to upset me. Your Satan judgement was made before you came to earth as an illegal immigrant and is irreversible. However, your followers must repent and follow God's Ten Commandments. They must forgive, love, have faith and believe in God which is the key to Heaven.

342. **Q: OK. What about Satan's followers?**

A: Tell them to repent and have faith in God and Lord Jesus.

343. **Q: Is that all?**

A: If they can do that it will satisfy God, but knowing your follower's dirty tricks, you must also prove to God and show your repentance by your deeds.

You must also accept Jesus as the Son of the living God and that Christ died for the ungodly people/souls.

344. **Q: So, what happens if I do not believe in Jesus?**

A: As a Christian you must give yourself completely to have a better chance to be saved by God in Jesus's name.

345. **Q: James, what is this nonsense that you must confess?**

A: Everybody knowingly or unknowingly is to worship to let go of sin. The Holy book stated clearly you must sincerely confess with your heart to come out of your mouth.

346. **Q: Are you making this up?**

A: No. The Holy Bible says Jesus is the Lord and believe in your heart that God raised him from the dead (or God could or did raise him), then you will be saved in the name of Jesus Christ. (Romans 8:1, 11)

347. **Q: Who introduced confession anyway?**

A: Jesus introduced it for forgiveness of sin.

348. **Q: What are different types of confession?**

A: There are four main sacraments: 1. Sacrament of reconciliation – means Jesus Christ wants us to reconcile with God the father; 2. Sacrament of penance – for example, Satan's followers realise how foolish and selfish that Satan was leading them to Hell, so they turned back to God. Satan: "James show respect for me, remember I was once God's Arch Angel." What other confession? 3. Confession – when we admit and confess speaking with our mouths and hearts; 4. Pardon and peace – whereby we ask God to forgive and grant our soul peace.

349. **Q: Why do you lie to people, why not admit that confession is an excuse to be forgiven and then a few minutes later you commit sin?**

A: Satan I don't take you seriously. We suffer daily of the weakening effect of original sin despite being baptised. If you read the Bible (Romans 7:15) St. Paul said, "For that which I do. I allow not: for what I would, that I do not, but what I hate, that I do I."

350. **Q: James, we all know your God is very jealous and always puts conditions on what he gives, so what is the condition for God to accept confession?**

A: There are only three simple conditions.

Satan (interrupts) "I told you there were conditions!!!"

Shush, Satan! 1. There must be acknowledgement of sin to be confessed; 2. Willingly wholehearted to repent the sin; 3. You must demonstrate sincerity and firm willingness to change and accept God's help.

351. **Q: I understand there are different types of sin, which determines which Heaven or Hell one goes (Islamists believe)?**

A: Minor sins are called venial, such as telling your secretary to tell the person on the phone that you were out when in fact you were not.

Mortal sins are more serious or grave, which does harm to us or others resulting in affecting one's relationship with God.

352. **Q: Tell me more about mortal sin.**

A: 1. A mortal sin must be serious enough that it breaches one or more of the Ten Commandments; 2. One must acknowledge that he or she is actually committing a serious or mortal sin such as armed robbery, which of course is a pre-meditated sin; 3. If the sin has one's full consent with your willpower and knowing the consequences.

353. **Q: Why should people forgive or confess anyway?**

A: Read Isaiah Chapter 1:18 "Come now, and let us reason together, saith the Lord, though your sins be as scarlet, they shall be as white as snow, though they be red like crimson, they shall be as wool."

354. **Q: We have heard so many times that Jesus spent three days after his death to bury all our sins in Hell and that we are now righteous forever whatever we do, it does not matter. Is it not true, James?**

A: Trust you to take words or phrases that suit you to argue about.

Jesus was aware that the original sin would continue to hunt us, but if we confess and acknowledge our sin then we shall be forgiven.

355. **Q: So, who will forgive the sinners? Fathers of Catholics, which some are worse than me (Satan)?**

A: You are Father of Lies, evil, so no one can be worse than you. After the resurrection, Jesus breathed and gave power to the apostles to forgive sins.

Look at John 20:23, "Whosoever sins ye remit, they are remitted unto them and whosoever sins

117

retain, they are retained." This power of forgiveness is passed to God's chosen leaders.

356. **Q: Can one pay through the post for the priest to forgive sinners?**

A: No – money is an earthly thing, which God is not interested to use to buy forgiveness.

357. **Q: What did the Bible say about sin?**

A: Read Jeremiah 17:9 "The heart is deceitful above all things and desperately wicked, who can know it? What causes sin is our personality and nature. This is the main root of our sins."

Mark 7:21 "For from within, out of the heart of men proceed evil thoughts, adulterers, fornication, murder, malice, deceit, lewdness, slander, arrogance, theft, etc."

The fact is, you cannot truthfully say, my heart is pure, I am clean without any sin. If you can then you are defiled. If not then you are heading to Hell, unless you repent now.

358. **Q: What about Satan's followers who have heard God, but ignore his commandment?**

A: Refer to Psalm 7:11 "God judged the righteous and God is angry with the wicked every day." Your people (Satan) are lawlessness who constantly worship god of sin, disobey him. God is very serious and ready to act, even death. Read Psalm 7:12, 13.

359. **Q: Will that be the end of sin if the person died?**

A: No. The biggest punishment for who God kills will come to you on the Day of Judgement – Romans 14:12, "So then everyone of us shall give account of himself to God."

Satan, you and your people are classified as a defiant lawbreaker.

360. **Q: James, God did not tell me what Hell will be like – will you come with us?**

A: I hope not. You are assured for everlasting destruction over so many years punishment in Hell. Hell will be fair according to the severity of your sin, because God is just. There is no way you can (sin) escape God's wroth.

Hell is not imaginal, it is factual. It is a place nobody wants to go as it is extremely fearful – worse than a fiery furnace, weeping, intense fire, which cannot be extinguished – 24-hours, 365 days and continual. In short, Hell is the Final Destination and you will taste more punishment (horror) than the sin.

361. **Q: Why did god just decide to do this to his creation – humans?**

A: God has not just decided. Read Genesis 3:8, 3:6, 2:17 and Romans 5:12.

God warned man they would die if they disobeyed God.

362. **Q: What does God mean by man will die?**

A: Man will die first spiritually and if the sin continues without repenting then a physical death follows, plus going to Hell after Judgement Day.

363. **Q: In short how will you, James, describe God?**

A: Omnipotent, sovereign, Alpha and Omega, Just, Holy, independent, eternal, spirit, one person, loving. (Jeremiah 10:10; Isaiah 44 and 6; John 1:1; 4:25; Psalm 90:2; Act 17:28; Romans 11:13; Exodus 15:11)

364. **Q: Why does your God who you describe as loving, slow to anger and quick to forgive, allow suffering?**

A: In a short answer, it is you who caused all this. There are many causes, but I wish to make it clear that God never willingly causes suffering but may allow suffering to use the situation to bring about some good.

365. **Q: Name some examples.**

A: Job, Joseph, Jonah, Daniel, Egypt, James Safo, or prison or serious illness to avoid death.

366. **Q: What other reasons?**

A: 1. Suffering could be a natural disaster such as earthquake, volcanoes, flood, fire, hailstones; 2. Human beings under the influence of Satan brings suffering, using our free will; 3. Human beings suffering upon ourselves.

367. **Q: Do you agree, James, with suffering?**

A: Yes, because how could humans learn from experience to be mature and balanced without suffering, by so doing, one learns from our mistakes, from the blunder then becomes wiser.

368. **Q: Don't you think God sits down and laughs at our suffering?**

A: No. God is not like you (Satan) who laughs after knowing you lead someone to do evil and he is caught. He is always at hand if we choose his way.

369. **Q: Why do humans make mistakes?**

A: God has given humans freedom of choice to make crucial decisions which sometimes leads to disaster or to do things his way – this is love for you. The influence of evil in human consciousness contributes to vulnerability to act against god's commandment.

370. **Q: Does God dislike sinners?**

A: God does not have a problem with sinners but dislikes the deliberate sinners. The reason is that these major sinners do not have the intention of stopping to sin. They think it is a game.

371. **Q: How can we experience God's loving presence in us?**

A: Start by believing in God's existence and experience his presence.

372. **Q: What is this nonsense of Jesus saying you must be born again?**

A: This was a parable Jesus used to answer Nicodemus, "I tell you the truth, unless you are born again, you cannot see the Kingdom of God" – Satan read John 3:3–8.

373. **Q: When does a person start a Spiritual Journey?**

A: When you accept Jesus God then you are at the beginning of God's kingdom and accept sincerely with your heart coincides with a spiritual journey.

374. **Q: Why does God force his desire on humans?**

A: No God never forces humans to follow or believe in him, hence humans have the choice to accept God's ways or reject God's ways and the consequences for humans.

375. **Q: Do Catholics always have to go to a priest to confess?**

A: If it is a serious sin then yes. If minor, you can say this in your heart and mouth, "I confess to almighty God, and to you, my brothers and sisters that I have greatly sinned in my thoughts and in my words, in what I have done and in what I have failed to do, through my fault, through blessed Mary ever-virgin, all the Angels and Saints and you, my brothers and sisters to pray for me to the Lord our God."

376. **Q: Why do Roman Catholics pray to Mary, Saints and Angels?**

A: No, we do ask Mary the mother of God, the son, the Angels, Saints, Holy Spirit to form interminably to pray to God the father, for us. Read the Apostles.

377. **Q: What did Jesus think of evil?**

A: In John 3:16-21, there are people who hate the light and will not come to be righteous. These people love darkness and evil.

378. **Q: What did Jesus say about the afterlife?**

A: Luke 16:19-31, Jesus said, there will be two after death (afterlife).

379. **Q: What did Jesus say about those seeking to go to Heaven?**

A: Jesus said the path to Heaven is narrow and only a few will find it after they have struggled with hardship and fasting or self-denial.

380. **Q: Does God know in advance what will happen to humans?**

A: Yes, He does.

381. **Q: What did Jesus say about reincarnation?**

A: In Matthew 22:30-33, He said "...dead people were certainly not dead but still living."

Mormonism

382. **Q: What is another name for Mormonism?**

A: The church of Jesus Christ of Latter-Day Saints

383. **Q: When and where was it founded?**

A: It was founded in the nineteenth century in America

384. **Q: According to LDs 2013 statistical report, how many members are there worldwide?**

A: 15.1 million members and continues to grow.

385. **Q: What is their nickname and why?**

A: Their nickname is "Mormons" or LDs which stands for Latter-Day Saints.

386. **Q: What is the Mormons' Holy Book and what does it contain?**

A: Their Holy book is called "Book of Mormons" and contains the testament of Jesus Christ.

387. **Q: Who founded the church and when?**

A: It was founded by Joseph Smith in (1805–1844).

388. **Q: Describe one important member of Mormon.**

A: Brigham Young migrated with many members and settled in Mid-West U.S.A. It is believed that they found Salt Lake City in one 1847 and spread their settlement.

389. **Q: Where are the headquarters of the Mormons?**

A: The headquarters is Salt City in USA.

390. **Q: Describe the hierarchy members.**

A: Mormons have a president who is considered as living the church's prophet, they have no professional clergy, the congregation is called WARDS. The congregation is led by Bishops and assisted by a priest.

391. **Q: Briefly describe the Book of Mormons.**

A: The book of Mormon was translated from an ancient record of prophets who inhabited America in the 19 centuries (compiled from their predecessors).

The book of Mormons has been translated into 82 languages. Members believe that the book of Mormons is the word of God and used with certain parts of the Bible in their teaching and that the book is another witness of Jesus.

392. **Q: What do Mormons think of the Bible?**

A: Mormons think there are parts of the Bible which are mistranslated.

393. **Q: What do they believe of the church and Bible?**

A: That the teaching of Jesus Christ's mission was re-introduced following the death of the early

Apostles which were not consistent with what Jesus taught. Mormons believe that these led to the church going astray from the truth.

394. **Q: What do Mormons think of their church and believe?**

A: That their church is a restoration of the real church organised by Jesus when he lived on Earth. Mormons also believe that there is an element of doubts in the Christian churches of the entire gospel of Jesus Christ.

They believe that faith in Jesus Christ is the first principle of the gospel, the first must be repentance of individual sin followed by baptism which must be in water/river/pool, etc. (immersion). This is done for forgiveness of sin.

395. **Q: What do Mormons think of God?**

A: That God has a glorified physical body and is the father of our spirit. That Jesus Christ was the son of God, through him alone can eternal happiness be found.

396. **Q: What is Mormons health code?**

A: These are abstaining from tobacco, consuming alcohol, tea, coffee, and the use of these were revealed to their prophets by God.

397. **Q: What is believed in gifts and revelations?**

A: Mormons believe in spiritual gifts and personal revelation in that individuals must be born again and to strive to abide by the Ten Commandments. These they believe will be fully effective in an individual's life.

398. **Q: How do they view fasting or abstaining from food and drink?**

A: Mormons are encouraged to fast one day a month usually the first Sunday of each month and to donate the money they save to charity or to assist the poor and the needy.

399. **Q: How do the church maintain?**

A: Mormons encourage tithing where members are encouraged to donate one tenth of their earning (income) to the church as its main source of income and there is no collection at their meetings.

400. **Q: Describe their charity duties.**

A: One of Mormons aims is charities which aim to carry out relief and development activities throughout the world.

401. **Q: What evidence support their charity work?**

A: In 2012 the Mormons records confirmed that Humanitarian effort including emergency response to about 52 countries, clean water projects in 36 countries wheelchair projects in 57 countries, Neonatal resuscitation training in 40 countries, eye care and equipment in 25 countries, immunisation programmes in 12 countries and food production and nutrition in 27 countries.

402. **Q: What day do they have worship?**

A: Mormons have command worship on Sundays which includes singing of hymns, prayers and talks on the gospel. They also build temples to receive ordinances. Married members are trained in Sunday school.

403. **Q: What is women's position in the church?**

A: Women hold leadership positions in the Church, give talks, read the gospel, but they are not ordained into the priesthood.

404. **Q: What other functions do ladies/women have?**

A: Relief society is a ladies' organisation and they aim to "increase faith and personal righteousness, strengthen families and homes and to provide relief by seeking out and helping those in need."

405. **Q: What is Mormons belief in marriage?**

A: Some of the early members of the church practice polygamy but this has since been discontinued. That marriage between man and woman is ordained by God. To have family and live everlasting. Mormons avoid abortion, unmarried sexual acts, no pornography which are regarded as sins and contrary to God's plan for individual happiness. Same sex marriage is not accepted but same gender attraction for people who are not practicing can be baptised in Mormons.

406. **Q: Name some famous Mormons.**

A: Mitt Romney (USA Politician) who in 2012 ran for USA Presidency. Pop star – The Osmond in 1970. Author of the Vampire themed Twilight series of novels, Stephen Meyer. Brandon Flowers, Frontman of rock group *The Killers* named his eldest son Ammon after a prophet from the book of the Mormon.

407. **Q: What do you think in this twentieth century people think of religion?**

A: There are some devoted worshippers of God, but young people feel being pressurised to attend God's house, hence when they reach an age they could refuse to attend. This misuse of drugs and alcohol and antisocial behaviour could be partly to blame.

Some religions are too sensitive to talk about it for fear of retribution, e.g. the Islamists.

408. **Q: Are there some countries to be credited of ancient religion?**

A: Some of the countries where faith started were either idol worshippers, especially before

Moses obtained the Ten Commandments from God (Mount Sinai) for the chosen people of Israel.

409. **Q: So how do we remember them?**

A: In Africa especially in Egypt, we know that the rulers "Pharaohs" were buried in special pyramids well before Jesus Christ was born. History states that the pyramids predate the birth of Jesus by about 3,000 years.

History also tells us that Jesus was taken to Egypt in fear of being killed by the king of Israel. Jesus spent most of his upbringing there until the king died.

Over the years death masks and paintings have been recovered from the Egyptian tombs, especially from a young Pharaoh Tutankhamen.

410. **Q: How do people know how to manage the dead?**

A: Managing the dead on their entombment was explained and the procedure in the Egyptian *Book of the Dead and Afterlife.*

411. **Q: Is there any information about South America?**

A: There appeared to be no written history and information is from researchers' archaeology.

There was evidence that the wealthy when they died were decorated with silver and gold stature relating to the gods they worshipped, especially the Mayans and the Aztec people.

Similar statues were found in Mexico in the region of Olmec's (1200 and 500 BCE).

412. **Q: What are some of the gods in South America?**

A: The god of the Olmec's was succeeded by the God Maya.

413. **Q: What did Mayan gods do?**

A: Human sacrifice was used for Mayan gods which featured animals and birds.

414. **Q: Who worshipped the sun?**

A: The Aztecs in about the twelfth century worshipped the sun and offered humans as a sacrifice. It was estimated that about 20,000 prisoners were offered to the sun.

The Inca were in Peru but were not worshippers like the Aztecs.

The moon was worshipped by some tribes in South America notably Chavin, Moche and Chimu. Roman Catholics were introduced in South America when the Spanish conquered.

415. **Q: What about Greece and Rome?**

A: It has been believed that civilization started in Greece. There were many gods, it was believed that through prayers and sacrifice, one could communicate with them, e.g. the Goddess Athena lived in the Parthenon in Athens.

There was a connection between the Romans and Alexandria in Egypt.

416. **Q: Where does one find the god with a horn?**

A: Celtic figure of god with a cruel human head cut off for sacrifice.

417. Q: In the Old Testament, what happened in Genesis?

A: A lot: God created the universe in six days; Cain killed his brother Abel; Noah and the Ark; building the Tower of Babel; God promised

Abraham; sacrifice of Isaac to God by Abraham halted; two sons of Isaac, Esau and Jacob; Pharaoh's dream; Moses killed Egyptians and fled; Moses led Israel out of Egypt, Moses brought the Ten Commandments from Mount Sinai to the Jews.

418. **Q: Which book covers the laws?**

A: Leviticus covers the laws and investiture duties for Israel.

419. **Q: Where can we read the Census of Israel?**

A: Numbers: Census of 12 tribes of Israel. Israel left Mount Sinai to desert wilderness. Israel rebelled against Moses and God. Israel was punished by an earthquake. Joshua was appointed as military commander.

420. **Q: In the book of Joshua, what happened?**

A: Moses died, Joshua succeeded him and sent spies to Canaan. Israel took over Canaan. Joshua died.

421. **Q: In the book of Judges, do they have courts to judge Judges?**

A: Prior to introducing Kingship, the rulers or leaders were called Judges, e.g. Judge Gideon, Samson.

422. **Q: Who was the great-great-grandmother of King David?**

A: Ruth – her rich widow died. She went to Naomi's house. Her son as Obed, he was King David's grandfather.

423. **Q: Who was the last great Judge?**

A: Samson, he lived with Prophet Eli after his mother promised God to do so.

424. **Q: Who anointed Saul as King?**

A: That was Samson.

425. **Q: Who defeated Philistine?**

A: David destroyed the giant Goliath.

426. **Q: Who was friend of David?**

A: King Saul's son, Jonathan.

427. **Q: Who succeeded King Saul and what terrible things did he do?**

A: David, but he caused adultery with Bathsheba, wife of Uriah. David sent Uriah to the front of the battlefield and was killed.

428. **Q: Who succeeded David?**

A: His son Solomon.

429. **Q: Who did God reveal the book of Psalms to?**

A: God revealed the Psalms to David for all of mankind.

430. **Q: What happened after David's death?**

A: Israel was broken into two kingdoms, Judah in the south and Israel in the north.

431. **Q: Who was the prophet during King Ahab of Israel?**

A: Prophet Elijah, one of the greatest prophets. He was taken to Heaven alive.

432. **Q: Who succeeded Elijah as prophet?**

A: Elisha.

433. **Q: Who was prophet during king Hezekiah's reign?**

A: The Great Prophet Isaiah.

434. **Q: Which two books were based on the earlier chapters of the Old Testament.**

A: 1st and 2nd Chronicles.

435. **Q: Which books dealt with the history of Judah and when did the Israelis return from exile?**

A: Ezra and Nehemiah.

436. **Q: Who was Nehemiah?**

A: He was a Jewish prophet who King Artaxerxes commissioned to supervise all of Jerusalem. He was then invited to rededicate Jerusalem by reading from the book of Moses.

437. **Q: Who was Esther?**

A: A beautiful Jewish woman who replaced the Queen at a banquet.

438. **Q: What makes Esther famous?**

A: She revealed that Haman forced the king to sign a decree to kill all the Jews and that she was also a Jew. The king hanged Haman and all the Jews were free of persecution.

439. **Q: Why do people always refer to Job?**

A: God allowed Satan to tempt him. He suffered terribly but never forsook God. At the end he was rewarded with twice as much as he had.

440. **Q: What do the Psalms consist of and who wrote them?**

A: It consists of songs, supplications, liturgical thanks given. Most of them were revealed to David by God or His angel.

441. **Q: Why are the Proverbs in the Bible?**

A: Stop playing daft. You should know better as God's ex-Arch Angel.

442. **Q: I am sorry, James. Your jealous God took away all the knowledge Satan had.**

A: I am extremely happy to hear this.

The Book of Proverbs consists of sayings about human behaviour, thoughts, purity in mind and thought, some short phrases, some were attributed to King Solomon.

443. **Q: Which author of the Old Testament claimed to be Solomon?**

A: Ecclesiastes who lectured about the nature of existence in God's universe and the value of eternity.

444. **Q: Where in the Bible do you find poetic dialogue between man and woman?**

A: Songs of Solomon. It was written in an erotic language referred to as daughters of Jerusalem.

445. **Q: Where do we find Judah destroyed?**

A: Prophet Isaiah's prophesy came true. Judah was destroyed but God punished Judah's enemies.

446. **Q: Where do we find the Babylonian Exile?**

A: Isaiah 40–50 covers all these.

447. **Q: Who wrote Isaiah 40–55?**

A: It was an anonymous prophet known as "Second Isaiah".

448. **Q: Where in the Bible do we find first, second and third of same prophet?**

A: This refers to Isaiah: it was believed that Isaiah 1–39 was himself, 40–55 by an anonymous prophet called Second Isaiah, Third Isaiah was 56–66; that is why Isaiah was divided into three.

449. **Q: Who prophesised the destruction of Israel after the Babylonian Exile?**

A: Prophet Jeremiah due to their religious and moral impurity.

450. **Q: What happened to Jeremiah for saying this?**

A: He was threatened, arrested and imprisoned until his prophesy came true, i.e. Israel was conquered by Babylon.

451. **Q: What happened to Jeremiah?**

A: He was taken to Egypt where his prophesy that Egypt would be invaded by Babylon came true.

The contribution of Prophet Jeremiah accounted for Israel's suffering.

452. **Q: What did Prophet Ezekiel do?**

A: His prophesy came true. He spoke against the wickedness and idolatry of Israel, he predicted it fell but then had a vision that all the dead bones rose from the dead, acquired new flesh and regained Israel from its enemies.

453. **Q: Which prophet refused to worship King Nebuchadnezzar's golden idol?**

A: Daniel and his three friends.

454. **Q: What happened to the three friends?**

A: Daniel's three friends – Shadrach, Meshach and Abednego were thrown into a blazing furnace, but they survived (God's miracle).

455. **Q: What was the interpretation of the king's dream by Daniel?**

A: Which one?

456. **Q: The writing on the wall.**

A: The king dreamt of mysterious writing appearing on the wall of the banqueting hall.

457. **Q: That is it – what is the interpretation?**

A: Daniel interpreted the death of King Belshazzar's and the empire's fall to the Persians and Medes.

458. **Q: What happened when Daniel refused not to obey King Darius and continued to pray to God Almighty?**

A: He was thrown to the lion's den but was saved by God.

459. **Q: Which prophet did God ask to marry a prostitute?**

A: Prophet Hosea – God told him to love her.

460. **Q: Why...that's crazy? (this question is from Satan)**

A: To demonstrate how God loves the Israelites despite their sin.

461. **Q: Come on, explain this further (another Satan question)?**

A: It is a parable of God's relationship with the Israelites, God is husband. His groom becomes faithless, corrupt, but repented and God had them back as lovers do.

462. **Q: What do we know about Prophet Joel?**

A: God promised through Joel to inform Judah that the Plague of Locusts would go, and he would restore prosperity.

463. **Q: What does it really mean?**

A: It was a sign of how God can destroy you and your followers (Satan) and how those who repent may go to Heaven.

464. **Q: Who was king of where Prophet Amos lived?**

A: Prophet Amos was around 786BCE.

465. **Q: What did Amos do?**

A: Prophet Amos warned both Judah and Israel to stop their corruption, fornication, faithlessness and living in ostentatious luxury.

466. **Q: He told them the consequences of punishment on judgement day and promised of Paradise for those who were righteous. Which is the shortest Old Testament?**

A: Prophet Obadiah – Destruction of Jerusalem 5876BCE. But Israel will be restored.

467. **Q: Who was the wisest prophet who wanted to be with me (Satan) but God stopped him?**

A: Jonah, but he was not the wisest prophet and not your follower. He was thrown into the deep sea, but the big fish brought him ashore to fulfil God's mission, which showed that nobody can escape God's plan.

468. **Q: Did Prophet Micah have enough to do?**

A: He also prophesised the destruction of northern and southern Israel, but God would restore it after their repentance.

469. **Q: Who was Nahum?**

A: He was a poetic prophet who was happy when Nineveh was destroyed and predicted the restoration of Judah and Israel.

470. **Q: Which of the prophets complained to God for not punishing my people?**

A: Prophet Habakkuk did complain about God not punishing the lawless.

471. **Q: God does not like to be told, so what did God does?**

A: God listens to his people who pray sincerely to him. In this case, God assured Habakkuk of his revenge. In fact, Habakkuk went public to praise God.

472. **Q: What is credited to Zephaniah?**

A: He did prophesise the destruction of Judah and the exile of the people of Jerusalem, but God would restore the people of Jerusalem, he predicted joy and song of praise.

473. **Q: Which prophet was not happy of people living in nice houses?**

A: Prophet Haggai was upset because God's worship places were in ruin, while people lived in nice houses. He organised a party for repair and refurbishment.

474. **Q: Which prophet received a message of the coming of the Messiah and other visions?**

A: It was Prophet Zechariah. He also had a vision of restoration of the Promised Land, rebuilding of the Temple and apocalyptic – victory at last to Israel and God's happiness.

475. **Q: Who was the last prophet named in the Old Testament and what did he do?**

A: It was Prophet Malachi 475BCE. He spoke against corruption by the priesthood leading people astray and predicted punishment on the way, he also predicted that Elijah would appear to turn people to God.

476. **Q: In the Old Testament, who were the two great powers during Abraham about 2000–1750?**

A: Egypt and Mesopotamia.

477. **Q: Who do some people pray to the Saints, e.g. prayer to St. Joseph by Divine Mercy, publication in Dublin.**

A: It would be ok to ask righteous people, e.g. saints, prophets or Jesus to intercede for you. Even Jesus said pray to God or ask him to pray for you. Prophets or saints never gave any form of intension for anyone to pray to them for their needs.

478. **Q: Is there more evidence Jesus was not God?**

A: The disciples asked Jesus how to teach them how to pray he taught them, "Our Father who art in heaven." This confirms that we are all children of God.

479. **Q: What was the meaning of when Jesus stated that he was the word?**

A: The meaning of this verse was that Jesus's teaching was the Word and if one did not follow what he was teaching, then it would be difficult to go to the Father. The statement could apply to any messenger of God who was teaching or revealing God's word. For example, Prophet Muhammad, Lord Krishna, Guru Nanak, etc.

could also have used these sentences or statements.

480. **Q: What does it really mean when in St. John 10:38 Jesus said, "I and my Father are one."**

A: Here, Jesus was telling the people that His teaching was consistent with the Almighty God. Similarly, other prophets could use the same phrase. For example, the revelation of the Ten Commandments to Moses (which is in the Quran), the revelation of the Quran to Prophet Muhammad, the revelation of the Psalms (which are scattered in the Quran) to David. All of them were gods and hence, God and "named prophet" are one.

481. **Q: How does one know Jesus was not God?**

A: In St. John 17:23 it says, "He who believes in me believes not in me but in Him who sent me." This is clear that Jesus was a messenger.

482. **Q: How is eternal life portrayed in the Christian world?**

A: Refer to St. John 17:3, Jesus said, "That they know thee, the only one true God and Jesus whom thou have sent."

483. Q: What did St. James 2:19 say about God?

A: You believe that God is one? You do well. Even the demon's shudder.

484. **Q: Will man see God?**

A: Blessed are the pure in heart, for they shall see God. (Matthew 5:8) Also John 4:22, John 14:1–6.

485. **Q: Who is in Heaven?**

A: For Christians' Heaven, God and Jesus will be there. (1 John 3:2; Revelation 22:3–4) From the Muslim perspective, God and all the angels and some of the prophets' spirits will be there.

486. **Q: Where in the Bible can we find drunkenness?**

A: Galatians 5:19–21; Ephesians 5:5–7.

487. **Q: Is there alcohol in Christians Heaven?**

A: No – nor meat nor drink but righteousness, peace and joy in the Holy Ghost. (Romans 14:17; Matthew 26:26–29; 1 Timothy 5:23)

In Christian Heaven, there is water of life, not rivers of wine. (Revelation 21:6–8, 22:1–2)

488. **Q: What has God prepared for Christian Heaven?**

A: Jesus' Heaven (1 Corinthians 2:9); Matthew 22:30; John 12:49–50).

489. **Q: What is the Christian marriage super?**

A: This can be found in Revelation 19:7–9. (Ephesians 5:25–32)

490. **Q: Jesus is reported to have come came as a spirit of God for all mankind but what were the Romans 8:9 discrimination by Paul?**

A: "If any man has not the spirit of Christ, he is none of his – even if he has well-known religion." Jesus is reported to have said that he came to divide but not to unite. This prophesy was evidence in current years.

491. **Q: Can anyone have the spirit of Christ even if he is not a Christian?**

A: If the person accepts Christ, yes – like Muslims they accept Christ, say 95% of the people I talk to.

492. **Q: John 1:12 stated that, "But as many as received him, to them gave power?"**

A: The power is a privilege, right, authority and with these powers one becomes the sons of God (also 2 Corinthians 1:22).

493. **Q: What does Psalm 32:1 mean by atonement (covering)?**

A: "Blessed is he whose transgression is forgiven whose sin is covered." This is covered by God or Jesus.

494. **Q: In Philippians 3:3–10 Apostle Paul gave a long speech/letter, thus he discriminated against some Christians who were not 100% Christians. Did any of the prophet followers behave in that way?**

A: Paul went from 100% against Christians to 100% supporter of Christ. He was a committed Christian. None of prophet's close friends deserted him.

495. **Q: Why did the prophesy in the Old Testament say a prophet would be born and named Immanuel?**

A: Immanuel means "God is with us".

The Bible refers to Jesus as the Word of God. (John 1:1, 14) In the Quran the angels said, "O Mary, God giveth thee glad tidings of a Word from Him. His name will be Christ Jesus the son of Mary."

496. **Q: Why is the Trinity proclaimed to be one with 1 + 1 + 1 = 3?**

A: Because God the Father, the son and Holy Spirit are one spiritually. One can say the Trinity is a spirit, soul and body; hence God can review himself in this Trinity.

497. **Q: What did the Angel say to Mary?**

A: In Luke 1:35 God sent the Angel Gabriel to announce to Mary, "The Holy Ghost shall come upon thee and the power of the Highest shall overshadow thee; therefore, also the Holy One which shall be born of thee shall be called the Son of God."

Comment: If one believes in Hindus Lord Krishna and believes in reincarnation then both Jesus and Krishna are attributes of God.

498. **Q: How did St. Paul add to the confusion of false prophet?**

A: Before Muhammad St. Paul warned, "But though we as an angel from Heaven preach any other gospel unto you than that which we have preached unto you let him be accursed." (Galatians 1:8)

"Thou art my beloved son; in thee I am well pleased." (Luke 3:22)

"Let God be true, but every man a liar." (Romans 3:4)

499. **Q: Are there evil spirits?**

A: We wrestle against flesh and blood but against the rulers of darkness of the world, against principalities, against spiritual wickedness in high places and therefore weapons of our warfare are not carnal (physical arm, cutlasses, swords, guns, knives, matches, petrol, bow and arrows), but mighty through God to the pulling down of a stronghold. (2 Corinthians 10:4; Ephesians 6:12)

500. **Q: But Christians worship Jesus Christ.**

A: No, Jesus could be a mediator/intermediary between man and God. But Christians do not worship Jesus. You can ask Jesus or any good prophet to pray to God for you.

501. **Q: Be honest, if Christians don't worship Christ why are the members called Christians after Christ?**

A: Satan you are talking nonsense again.

Chapter 4

Confucianism

502. **Q: What is Confucianism and which country?**

A: It is not a religion; their teaching is based on moral values and laws. Their aim is to perfect individual social, political and family stability – it originated in China.

503. **Q: When was it founded and by whom?**

A: It was founded by K'ung Fu in about 551–479BCE.

504. **Q: What does it mean i.e. Confucianism?**

A: Confucius's is the Latinisation of K'ung Fu Tu and means Master K'ung.

505. **Q: What did the ancient scholars do?**

A: The Chinese scholar called jau implemented the ritual of cult worship, making offerings to many gods, including Heaven and earth, but at the same time respect the tradition.

506. **Q: What other practices are there?**

A: They emphasise on good behaviour (Li) including: ceremonial duties, rituals, funerals, sacrifices, honesty and love which will result in spiritual development and moral growth.

507. **Q: What important thing happened in the Han Dynasty?**

A: They gathered ideas from other doctrines and determined the best i.e. Yin and Yang, these are valued in the world and history, plus the five elements.

508. **Q: Name the five elements.**

A: Earth, air, water, fire, wood (+ metal) using these to explain and act in mystical and prophetic terms.

509. **Q: What other faiths did they select doctrines from?**

A: Buddhism and Taoism, politics, ethics and literature to compare the way of life.

510. **Q: Name the six classics and what they stand for.**

A:

1. Shi Ching – poetry.

2. I Ching – changes.

3. Shu Ching – history.

4. Li Chi – rituals.

5. Ch'un-Chin – spring and autumn.

6. Yueh China – music.

511. **Q: What are these classics and other writings used for?**

A: These were combined to be the syllabus for schools and colleges and examinations were set based on these.

512. **Q: Name some establishments where they were used?**

A: Imperial College and the civil service during the Dan dynasty (206BCE to 220CE).

513. **Q: What aspect of religion is Confucianism?**

A: There is no religious connection, hence no church, no priest, no creed or dogma and no interest in God or gods.

514. **Q: What do they regard Confucius?**

A: Some worship his as Holy and Wise, supervisor being as Heaven and Earth. Hence, they pray to him and offer sacrifice to him/his name.

Chapter 5

Freemasonry

515. **Q: What is Freemasonry?**

A: Freemasonry is a peculiar system of morality, veiled in allegory and illustrated by symbols.

516. **Q: What do you mean by an "allegory"?**

A: An "allegory" is a figurative representation in which something else is intended than what is exhibited (painting and scripture), according to Nuttals Dictionary.

517. **Q: (a) What do you mean by "a system of morality"? (b) Why "peculiar"?**

A: "A system of morality" is a type of behaviour. The word "peculiar" is used in the meaning of "particular".

518. **Q: What are "symbols"? Give a Masonic example.**

A: A symbol is "an outward and visible sign of an inward and invisible truth".

For example: The "square" represents "matter" and the compass represents "spirit".

519. **Q: (a) Who are fit and proper persons to be made Freemasons? (b) What do you mean by "just", "upright", "free", "morals"?**

A: **(a)** The just, upright and free, of mature age and sound judgement. **(b)** "Just" is defined as agreeable to fact, or truth, or justice. "Upright" is defined as "comfortable to moral rectitude"; "free" means (physically) "unrestricted" and (mentally) "unbiased". "Morals" means "standards of behaviour".

520. **Q: What is the meaning of "Freemason": (a) Originally and (b) in speculative Masonry?**

A: **(a)** A "free" operative Mason is not bound to work in one locality. **(b)** A Speculative Mason has freedom of thought and is "soul-free".

521. **Q: (a) What are the distinguishing characteristics of every true Free and "Accepted Mason"? (b) What is the meaning of "Accepted Mason"?**

A: **(a)** The distinguishing characteristics of every true Free and Accepted Mason is virtue, honour and mercy. **(b)** "Accepted Masons" are men received into the mason's guild not as workers, but because of their interest in the teachings, secrets, ritual, symbolism and philosophy of the ancient Craft.

522. **Q: What are the "true and proper signs" by which to recognise a Freemason? Why?**

A: "All s…, 1…and p…" (secret), because these indicate the "perfect stone", capable of forming part of the wall of a Temple.

523. **Q: (a) What are the t…g… emblematical 1…s in Freemasonry? (b) What are they also called? (c) What does "L" stand for in V…s of s…L…? meaning?**

A: **(a)** The Volumes of the Secret Law, the square and the compass. **(b)** The "furniture" of the Lodge. In the temple of Humanity, for Furniture we have those qualities and faculties with which He endows all true Freemasons. **(c)** L…stands for "Lore", meaning wisdom (not law).

524. **Q: What are the 1...r L...s?**

A: **(a)** The W J W, situated in the South to represent the Sun and to rule the day. **(b)** The W S W situated in the West to represent the Moon and to rule the night. **(c)** The Right Worshipful Master situated in the East to rule and direct the Lodge and possess wisdom.

525. **Q: (a) What are the three great pillars on which a Lodge of Freemasons figuratively rests? (b) What great qualities are symbolised? (c) With what types of Architecture are they associated?**

A: **(a)** The three great pillars on which a lodge of Freemasons figuratively rests are typified by The Right Worshipful Master in the East whose pillar signifies wisdom (Ionic Order of Architecture). **(b)** The W S W in the West, whose pillar signifies strength (Doric Order of Architecture). **(c)** The W J W in the South, whose pillar signifies beauty (Corinthian Order of Architecture).

526. **Q: (a) What are the three grand principles on which the order is founded? (b) How are each of these emphasised in the ritual?**

A: **(a)** The three grand principles on which the order is founded are brotherly love, relief and truth. **(b)** Brotherly love is emphasised in the ritual where, after the investiture, the Right Worshipful Master says to the candidate, "Settle your differences amicably...then clothe yourselves, enter the lodge and work together with that love and harmony which should at all times characterise Freemasons."

Relief is emphasised in the "divested" candidate being asked to contribute to The Secretary Widows Trunk.

Truth is emphasised at the end of the charge in the First Degree: "You should more especially cultivate such of the liberal arts and sciences as may lie within the compass of your attainment; and, without neglecting the ordinary duties of your station in life, you should feel yourself called on to make a daily advancement in masonic knowledge".

527. **Q: What is the difference between a "lodge" and a "temple"?**

A: A lodge is "opened" or created in the "inner" worlds inside the physical temple: "The true Temple of Humanity, of which each Freemason lodge forms a part, is not erected in space and time". "…to the truly enlightened mason the sun never sets, for his real life is spent in the living temple where there is no darkness and where The Great Architect of the Universe is ever the light", and "The Universe is the Temple of Deity".

528. **Q: What is the extent of a lodge?**

A: "The extent of the Lodge, emblematical of the proportions of the Temple of Humanity; which is in length from East to West, in breadth from North to South, and in depth from the Zenith to the centre of the earth".

529. **Q: What is the correct shape of a temple? Why?**

A: The correct shape of a temple is a rectangle with one pair of sides twice that of the other pair. This forms two adjacent squares, representing "as above, so below".

530. **Q: Why are lodges situated due E-W?**

A: Because in masonry the Deity as wisdom is symbolised by the sun, which rises in the East where the R W M (who symbolises wisdom) is therefore placed and reaches its greatest strength in the South (in the Northern hemisphere) where the W J W, who symbolises beauty, is placed. Also, as the 1 T B points out, all sacred Buildings were oriented E-W, including King Solomon's Temple.

531. **Q: (a) Why do lodges stand on holy ground?**

A: **(a)** Our lodges stand on holy ground because they form part of the Temple of Humanity and because of their consecration to highest ends...and will become increasingly holy in so far as the brethren working therein are actuated by the sincere desire to benefit humanity. **(b)** Therefore, when setting up the temple and when

166

moving about in the temple after it has been set up, our thoughts should be on high masonic ideals and NO mundane conversation should take place in the temple. Some lodges lock the door of the temple once it is set up and all lodges have an outer guide with sword and inner guide with hammer.

532. **Q: What is the "summit" of the profession of Freemasonry?**

A: "The summit of the profession of Freemasonry is, figuratively speaking, an ethereal mansion, veiled from mortal eyes by the starry firmament and depicted in our lodges by seven stars. To reach this canopy we have the assistance of a ladder…this ladder has as many staves or rounds as comprise all the virtues, but three are principal – faith, hope and charity."

533. **Q: Where are the following "lights" and what do they represent? (a) The 5-pointed star; (b) The 6-pointed star; (c) The 7-pointed star**

A: **(a)** The 5-pointed star is found in the East behind the R W M. It represents the Perfect Man who has five senses, five fingers on each hand, five toes on each foot, etc. **(b)** The 6-pointed Star, represented by two interlaced triangles, is found in the ceiling of the temple above the altar. It is illuminated and has the letter G in its centre. This G in the centre stands for "Gnomon" – the Greek for "manifested God". It represents God manifest in His universe – the triangles of spirit and matter being completely interlaced. **(c)** The 7-pointed star is depicted in the T B at the top of the ladder from the altar. It represents (secret).

534. **Q: What is the shape of the altar and what does it represent?**

A: The shape of the altar should be a double cube, either standing upright or lying on its side. It represents God reflected in matter. "As above, so below".

535. **Q: What is the meaning of: (a) The circle on the altar in the T B? (b) The two parallel lines?**

A: **(a)** "In all regularly constituted lodges, there is a point within a circle round which a mason cannot err." **(b)** The circle is bounded by two grand parallels between North and South, one representing Moses (law) and the other King Solomon (wisdom). On the upper part rests the V...s of the S... L... In going around the circle we must necessarily touch on both those parallel lines as well as the V-S -L; while a mason keeps himself thus circumscribed, he cannot err.

536. **Q: What is the zymology of the alter light?**

A: The ruby-coloured altar light (which should be on a pedestal close to the altar or suspended on a pulley from the ceiling) is emblematical of the sacred fire which is ever-burning at the heart of all creation. Hence it is lit (by a Past Master) before the brethren enter the temple and extinguished after they leave.

537. **Q: What are the "Jewels" of a lodge and their symbolical meaning?**

A: The Jewels of a lodge are of two kinds: **(a)** The moveable jewels, the s..., the l... and the p... r..., appear on the collars of the three principle officers and are transferred to successors to the officers on the day of installation. **(b)** The immovable jewels lie open in the lodge for the brethren to moralise upon. They are: **(1)** The tracing board, which is a picture with masonic symbols upon which to moralise; **(2)** The rough ashlars, a rough cubical stone near to the W J W, representing the rough nature of the Enter Apprentice not yet capable of fitting into the temple wall; **(3)** The smooth ashlars, a smooth polished cubical stone near the W S W, representing the polished nature of the FC capable of fitting into the temple of humanity. "In the Temple of Humanity, the jewels are those individuals that have been prepared and polished so that they reflect the divine nature".

538. **Q: What is the meaning of "Ornaments" of a lodge and their symbolical meaning?**

A: The "Ornaments" of a lodge are: **(a)** The mosaic pavement, symbolising spirit and matter; **(b)** The b… s…, ever reminding us of the presence of God in His universe (six-pointed star); **(c)** The indented border of the pavement, consisting of alternate black and white triangles.

The apex of each white triangle facing outward, thus representing the inner guardian wall of spirit protecting manifestations. In the Temple of Humanity, the ornaments may be said to be the beauty shed abroad by T G An O T U".

539.   **Q: What asymbologies do you ascribe to the four Tassels?**

A: These are four Tassels "pendent to the four corners of the Lodge" and depicted on the mosaic pavement. They have many symbolic meanings, e.g. earth, air, fire and water and masonic ally – the four virtues of temperance, fortitude, prudence and justice. These may be allocated as follows:

That in the North-West corner, the place of entry into a lodge, may be allocated to fortitude – the courage necessary to take the first step and to carry one along the way. The next tassel, in the North-East corner, is that of prudence and is next to the Senior Deacon representing the mind, which practices prudence to attain to wisdom. The third tassel in the South-East corner is that of justice and is next to the Director of Ceremony who "sees that everything is done in order". The fourth tassel, in the South-West is near to the Junior Deacon representing the emotions and hence is temperance.

540. **Q: A lodge must be "just, perfect and regular". What does this mean?**

A: **(a)** A lodge is "just" when the charter is present. **(b)** A lodge is "perfect" when there are seven duly constituted Masons present. **(c)** A lodge is "regular" when it has been duly convened by a notice of meeting with agenda.

541. **Q: As "man is made in the image of God", explain the zymology of the lodge as man.**

A: **(a)** One interpretation of the zymology of the officers of the lodge are its prevalence in the male craft, e.g. the Right Worshipful Master represents spirit, the Worshipful Senior Warden represents soul and the Worshipful Junior Warden represents body. **(b)** A fuller interpretation of the lodge officers representing man is that the three Chief Officers represent the triune spirit in man, namely the Right Worshipful Master represents love-wisdom the Worshipful Senior Master represents will the Worshipful Junior Warden represents higher mind – the creative abstract mind. These "rule" the personality consisting of:

Senior Deacon, the lower, concrete mind "near the Right Worshipful Master".

Junior Deacon, the emotions, "near the Worshipful Senior Warden".

Inner guild, the vital etheric body "within the entrance of the lodge". The outer guild is the physical body, which guards the inner man, the true self.

542.   **Q: (a) Give the order of the procession. (b) Why do we not just go in singly? (c) Why do we "square the lodge" with the left foot? (d) Why do we always go around the lodge? clockwise? (e) Why do we salute the pedestals?**

A: **(a)**   Thurifer   Secretary

Director of Ceremony	Orator
Enter Apprentice's	Past Masters of the Lodge
Visiting Enter Apprentice	Bro 30'
Fellow Craft's	Visiting Bro 30'
Visiting Fellow Craft's	Bro 32'
Master Mason's	Visiting Bro 32'
Visiting Master Mason's	Bro 33'
Bro 18'	Visiting Bro 33'
Visiting Bro 18'	Junior Warden
Visiting Past Master's	Senior Warden
Inner Guild	Immediate Past Master

Almoner   Right Worshipful
                           Master with
                           Deacons

                Treasurer

(b) We go in together because we work as a
group and not singly. **(c)** We "square the lodge"
with the left foot at the corners to mark out the
rectangular "foundation" of our lodge. **(d)** We
always work clockwise because of our solar inner
symbology and hence we follow the "apparent"
movement of the Sun from East to West. **(e)** We
"salute" the pedestals because thus we
symbolically recognise and accept the rule of the
triune spirit in our lives when "the lodge is open",
i.e. the spirit is manifest.

543. **Q: (a) Give the order of the censing and the
      number of swings. (b) What is the use of the
      incense?**

      A:

      a. **Right Worshipful Master:** 3, 3, 3; 3 to left and
         right, seven circles; Altar

b. **Worshipping Junior Warden:** 3, 1, 1; 3 to left and right, seven circles

c. **Worshipping Senior Warden:** 3, 3, 1; 3 to left and right, seven circles

d. **Junior Deacon:** 1, 1, 1

e. **Senior Deacon:** 3, 1

f. **Visitors:** 33' – 3, 3, 3, 32', 31' 30 – 3, 3, 1 18', visiting Past Master's – 3, 1, 1

g. **Immediate Past Master:** 3, 3, 3, 1

h. **Orator:** according to rank

i. **Past Masters of the Lodge:** 3, 1, 1

j. **Director of Ceremonies AND Columns:** One each

k. **Inner Guild:** 1, 1

l. **Outer Guild:** 1

m. **(b)** The use of incense is to help purify and raise the vibrations of the inner man, different perfumes affect the emotions differently.

544. **Q: (a) What is the order of lighting the candles and compared with the order of censing? (b) Why does the Senior Deacon perform this? function?**

A: **(a)** The order of lighting the candles is: Right Worshipful Master – Worshipping Senior Warden, Worshipping Junior Warden. The order of censing is: Right Worshipful Master – Worshipping Junior Warden – Worshipping Senior Warden. **(b)** The Senior Deacon performs this function because he represents man's mind with which he works in manifestation. "As a man thinketh in his heart, so is he."

545. **Q: What is the difference between a r… s… p and a p…s…p, and what are their inner significances?**

A: The r…s…p is always taken before giving the s…n. It symbolises moving from the square of "matter" into the triangle of spirit. The p…s…ps are taken when advancing to the altar and represent advancing through the three "form" planes, enteric, emotional and mental, to the spiritual plane.

546. **Q: What is the significance of the W… T…s? What do they have in common with the p…s…ps?**

A: The significance of the W T's is that they link the operative and speculative crafts by showing how the tools used by an operative Enter Apprentice can be symbols of the qualities needed by a speculative Mason to shape his character. Note that they are all based, in construction, on a straight line and that they share this with the p...s...ps.

547. **Q: What is the full symbology of the apron?**

A: The symbology of the colour of the apron is given in the ritual but the shape is also important as it represents the triangle of spirit not yet manifested in the square of matter.

548. **Q: What is for you, the most important aspect of Freemasonry?**

A: Of course, being part of Masonry with like-minded people and sharing with them the mysteries and symbolism. This is reflected in the many married women whose husbands are in the UGLE and Grand Lodge of Ireland, where sharing the same tenets of Masonry enriches their family life. It is certainly the brotherly love and companionship. I see Freemasonry as an opportunity for enhancement and development of one's inner-self. There is no material gain about it; it is purely a system supporting the process of striving for perfection and awareness of oneself.

549. **Q: What is the main difference (apart from the admission of women) between the United Grand Lodge of England and Co-Freemasonry?**

A: We are an international order operating in 62 countries in the world, and all the Federations in the individual countries are responsible for their own administration. Another difference between ourselves and the United Grand Lodge of England is that we work all the degrees to the 33rd Degree. There is no separation between the craft and the higher degrees. We work not through Provincial Grand Lodges but rather through to the 31st and 32nd degrees. Very few people ever reach the 33rd degree. However, as Most Puissant Grand Commander and

Representative to the Supreme Council, the responsibilities carry with them the 33 rd degree. Other members of this degree constitute the Grand Council. Our Grand Secretary is a 32 nd degree, and a member of the Consistory Council, which is responsible for the administration of our Federation.

550. **Q: Do you think that the fact that Co-Freemasonry is recognised by the irregular Masonic bodies in Europe and elsewhere makes it unlikely that it will ever be recognised by the United Grand Lodge of England?**

A: Although we are not recognised by the UGLE, we do follow in this country the same tenets. That is, brotherly love, relief and truth. We do not recognise all Masonic organisations, and as representative of the Supreme Council I must hold a list of these bodies in fraternal relations, and only their members would be able to participate in our meetings.

551. **Q: Do you think the fact that the headquarters are in Paris ultimately makes Co-Freemasonry unattractive to the English-speaking world? Or, are there many lodges in the States, Australia and New Zealand for example?**

A: No, I don't think that makes a lot of difference. There are many lodges in Australia, the States, New Zealand, also in South Africa and India. Annie Besant (see Box) was initiated, passed and raised and elevated into all the higher degrees in Paris and brought Co-Freemasonry to England in 1902. After which she took it to all parts of the British Empire and the United States.

552. **Q: Would you say that Co-Freemasonry is more esoterically oriented than the United Grand Lodge of England?**

A: Yes, I imagine so, but it is difficult to answer as I can only answer for Co-Freemasonry. It could be that this is so because there is no separation between the craft and the higher degrees.

The esoteric and symbolic studies in the craft are developed by progression into the higher degrees. We have an extensive library on esoteric subjects, from which members can borrow books. Non-members are welcome to use it too if for the purposes of study, subject to prior appointment. Co-Freemasonry is very esoterically oriented, partly because the order was founded in England by Annie Besant, a member of the Theosophical Society. Today we still have many members of the Theosophical Society and we all benefit from Annie Besant's legacy.

553. **Q: Do people who join Co-Freemasonry go on to join other organisations, such as Martinis or Rosicrucian bodies?**

A: I think it is more the other way around. We find that many people come to us from other organisations. And of course, as I already mentioned, we work the Rose Croix degree. Before admitting members from other organisations, we ascertain that they are no longer members of other Masonic bodies.

554. **Q: What are the number of lodges and how many people approximately constitute the British Federation?**

A: The headquarters of the order are in Paris, where representatives of the federations meet at least three times a year. In the British Federation, the Most Puissant Grand Commander is representative to the Supreme Council in Paris. I am responsible for a Grand Council of the 33rd degree, the Consistory Council and 23 craft lodges, as well as four Mark lodges, three Holy Royal Arch Chapters, seven Rose Croix Chapters, one Knights Kadosh of the 30th degree, one Knights Templar Preceptor and priory, as well as the 31st 32nd and 33rd degrees, which are also worked ceremonially. Some lodges and chapters follow the rituals of the English masculine obedience's. We have currently approximately 450 members.

Most of the lodges are based in Surbiton. But we have lodges in Tunbridge Wells, Bristol, Lees, Blackburn, Norwich, Birmingham, Northampton, Letchworth, Camberley, Southsea, Croydon and Northern Ireland. The Supreme Council is in Paris because Mlle Maria Deraismes and Georges Martin founded the Supreme Council there. The order was organised in such a way that the Supreme Council would remain in Paris and has done so except when France was occupied during the war years when the authority of the Supreme Council was vested in the British Federation.

555. **Q: Do you communicate with the Grand Orient of France?**

A: Yes, we are in fraternal relations with the Grand Orient and, in fact, a lodge of that order has met in London for the past 100 years and meets now in Hexagon House.

556. **Jeanne Halewood, Grand Secretary of the Order, recently gave a lecture on Co-Masonry**

at the Canonbury Masonic Research Centre. She finished it with the following quote:

"I sought my soul but my soul I could not see
I sought my God, but my God eluded me
I sought my brother and I found all three."

557. **Q: By whom and when was the first list of General Regulation made and when was it approved?**

The first list of General Regulation was compiled by the Grand Master of England in 1720. It was approved in 1723.

558. **Q: Who and when were the landmarks of Freemasonry published and how many were accepted?**

Albert Gallatin McKay in 1858 wrote twenty-five landmarks but only seven were generally accepted and adopted by various lodges with slight adaptations according to the jurisdiction.

559. **Q: Name the seven Landmarks.**

Monotheism is the sole dogma of Freemason.

560. **Q: Which is the largest masonic temple?**

The most complex and largest masonic temple is the grandest temple in Detroit – which is 14 stories and holds about seven craft lodges.

561. **Q: Describe First Degree tracery boards.**
The ladder and three pillars symbolising humans place.

562. **Q: Describe Second degree tracing board.**
A spiral staircase leading to the interior of King Solomon's Temple.

563. **Q: Describe Third degree tracing board.**
A coffin signifies that when a true mason die, they go to a superior and richer place.

Chapter 6

564. **Q: Who formed the Hare Krishna movement or society of for Krishna Consciousness?**

A: The movement was inspired by Chaitanya, a sixteenth century mystic from Bengal (who was said to be an incarnation of Krishna).

565. **Q: How was it spread to the East?**

A: In the 1920s the leader of the movement instructed a follower to take his teaching to the West (English-speaking world).

566. **Q: What resulted from this instruction?**

A: In 1965 Prabhupada went to the USA and founded ISKLON "The International Society for Krishna Consciousness" and many non-Indians were attracted to Hinduism.

567. **Q: What are the followers of Krishna devoted to?**

A: They are devoted to chanting Krishna's name, renouncing violence, gambling, alcohol and illicit sexual relationships.

568. **Q: How does one define Hinduism?**

A: Because of the wide array of practice and belief, founded within it, it is not easily defined.

569. **Q: Which country has the majority of Hindus?**

A: India where there are about 80% are Hindus.

570. **Q: Who founded Hinduism?**

A: There was no single founder.

571. **Q: Is there single scriptures or commonly agreed sets of teachings?**

A: No. Over the centuries, there have been key figures teaching different philosophies and numerous holy books.

572. **Q: What is common then among Hindus?**

A: Writers often refer to Hinduism as "a way of life" or family religion who believe in Almighty God but not a single religion.

573. **Q: Where was the Hindu name derived from?**

A: Hindu was derived from the river Sindhu.

574. **Q: When did the term Hindu change to Hinduism?**

A: In true Hindu, this has not changed. It was only in the nineteenth century during the British colonialism and missionary activity that the suffix "ism" was added to be Hinduism.

575. **Q: What is the underlining feature of Hinduism?**

A: In fact, it is commonly agreed to be cultural political and geographical.

576. **Q: What common beliefs of Hindu do they share with other Indian religions?**

A: The concept of reincarnation or karma and samsara because Jains, Sikhs and Buddhism accept this teaching.

577. **Q: What does the Samsara belief mean?**

A: It is the continuous cycle of birth and reincarnation with favourable rebirth achieved by living well and achieving good karma, the moral law cause and effect.

578. **Q: In the reincarnation process, what is crucial?**

A: dharma.

579. **Q: What is dharma?**

A: It is the concept of the true moral path each Hindu must follow, what is right in rituals and everyday behaviour.

580. **Q: What is the ultimate goal of Hindus?**

A: Achieving Moksha.

581. **Q: What is Moksha?**

A: It is to be in a transcendent state, that is break out of the cycle of Samsara.

582. **Q: How do Hindus view life?**

A: To Hindus all life is sacred, so they avoid violence, and many are vegetarians.

583. **Q: Why do Hindus not eat cow?**

A: Because it means taking/killing the cow's life which is sacred. Cows provide milk to feed humans.

584. **Q: How may social classes are Hindus divided into?**

A: All Hindus are divided or born into one of the four social classes which collectively are known as vamas.

585. **Q: What are these classes and their meanings?**

A: The four traditional classes (vamas) are:

1. Brahman (the priestly class)
2. Vaishya (merchants and farmers)
3. Sudra (the lowest division)
4. Kshatriya (warriors).

586. **Q: How does the class system affect a Hindus' life?**

A: For Hindus, the cast of birth affects the person's choice of marriage partner, including whom you may eat and accept food with.

587. **Q: Name three best known Hindu scriptures.**

A: 1. Mahabharata; 2. Bhagavad-Gita; 3. Ramayana.

588. **Q: Briefly describe Mahabharata.**

A: This tells of the power struggle between two rival families and with a vast cast of characters.

589. **Q: Briefly describe the Bhagavad-Gita Holy book.**

A: This is the most famous of the Hindu Holy books. It describes events before a great battle, introducing Krishna (avatar of the God Vishnu), explains the concept of dharma, the main theme is one of good triumphing over evil.

590. **Q: What is the Ramayana book?**

A: It is about poems of the God Rama and his wife Sita who were rescued by God Hanuman, that describes very real human emotions as the couple endured hardship and pain.

591. **Q: Describe the branch of Vaishnavites.**

A: These are Hindus who are devoted to worshipping Vishnu being the supreme God. It was believed that Vishnu gave life to the creator (known as Brahma) and Vishnu sustained and protected all that Brahma created.

Vishnu avatars include Rama and Krishna who are also worshipped by Hindus.

592. **Q: Briefly describe the branch Saivites.**

A: Saivites worship the God Siva, known as the "destroyer". He was regarded as the supreme God by the Saivites.

Siva was believed to have recreated whatever he destroyed and embraced other opposites (life and death, time and eternity).

593. **Q: What are the three main avatars of God's messengers?**

A: Brahma, Vishnu and Siva were known as three Gods of the Trimurti.

594. **Q: When these God messengers or Avatars come to earth, did they marry?**

A: Yes, they had consorts who were called Goddesses just like a wife of a king is called a queen or a prince's partner is called a princess or prophet's wives (Muhammad) is called "mother of faithful".

595. **Q: Who was the wife or consort of Vishnu?**

A: Lakshmi, she was known for her generosity and who valued social order and cleanliness.

596. **Q: Who was Brahma's wife or consort?**

A: It was goddess Saraswati who was popularly known as the goddess of the arts and she was believed to have made anything her husband thought of.

597. **Q: Who was Siva's wife?**

A: He took different forms including Parvai (gentle goddess) or the form of Kali (slayer of demons) and as Durga (able to destroy evil).

598. **Q: What do Hinduisms need for praying?**

A:

• Mala – Prayer beads (108 small beads).

• Murti – a statue, at least two inches in height or an image or photograph of the God Krishna or other Gods.

• Incense, sticks and holder.

- Small bell.
- Gita – Holy Book.

599. **Q: Name the months (approximate data) that Hindus celebrate specific festivals.**

A:

14 January	Makar Sankranti
17 February	Maha Shivaratri (day of fasting)
5 March	Holi (festival of colours)
28 March	Shri Rama Navami
14 April	Tamil New Year (celebrated by Tamil Hindu community)
29 August	Rakhee/Raksha Bandhan
4 September	Shri Krishna Janmashtami
13 October	Navarotri begins
20 October	Durgashtami
22 October	Vijayadashami – Navaratri ends

600. **Q: What will happen after death and does rebirth have any specific qualities?**

A: Hindus believe in reincarnation or life consists of a continuous cycle of birth, death and rebirth

Dharma (which is right or wrong in the specific circumstances). This varies for individual societies, social classes but there are Hindu values that are universal and widespread.

The rebirth does not guarantee any specific religion, sex, colour, IQ, social class.

601. **Q: What are Hindus social caste status system and describe the stages?**

A: There are four stages or statuses called the menu of human beings.

1. *Sutra:* role is to be a servant and to serve people. It is the lowest working class.
2. *Vaisya:* these are a higher class of merchants, farmers, weavers, landlords, etc.
3. *Kshatria:* the role of power, warrior, soldier or king.
4. *Brahmana:* volunteer, yogi, priest, helping the community welfare.

602. **Q: What are the holy texts of Hindus?**

A: The holy text is divided into two categories. "Sruiti or Heard" is the oldest of the two. This was because ancient sages went off to remote places to meditate aiming to perceive sacred truths. For example Veda which means knowledge and covers different areas of sacred knowledge and ritual. The second category is called Smruti meaning remembered. This refers to a vast number of epics, an Avola, for example Rama in Ramayana and Krishna in Mahabharata.

This category covers the whole range of human experience including love, war, politics, personal morality and religion.

603. **Q: What are the hymns, chants, rituals?**

A: Hindus hymns to the gods are Rig Veda. Chants are Sama Veda.

Rituals are Yajur Veda, rites and spells which especially deals with those concerned with healing known as Atharva Veda.

604. **Q: What is Upanishads in Hindus?**

A: Upanishads is an example of Holy text – sruti and it means "sitting down near to". It helps one to focus on Brahman and the relationships between individual souls and supreme God. This can be achieved by sitting down next to the guru (teacher) to learn their wisdom.

605. **Q: What is Aum?**

A: This is a sacred verbal syllable sounded at different levels. Hindus chant it as a means of meditating on the ultimate reality and connecting with the innermost self (Atma) and Brahman. The three levels or sounds A, U, M possesses a vibrational aspect apart from its conceptual significance. If pronounced correctly, the vibrations resonate through the body and penetrate the Atman.

Aum put individuals into a state of the cosmos, manifestation, maintenance and dissolutions. It also relates to the three aspects of Brahman who presided over these states: Brahma, Vishnu and Shiva. Hindus regard Aum as Trinity.

606. **Q: How do Hindus regard earthy things?**

Hindus regard a lot of earthly things as Holy and they worship them; for example, rivers, mountains, such as Mount Kailash and River Ganges represents the supreme god *Siva* and it

198

has been every Hindus' wish to die near the Ganges river or the mountain. A lot of Hindus make a will so that when they die their body is cremated and their ashes scattered on the river or mountain.

607. **Q: How do Hindus regard a pilgrimage?**

A: Hindus make a pilgrimage to sacred sites in the hope of cleansing themselves of sin and lessening their karmic debts.

608. **Q: What is Atman?**

A: The innermost self or transcendental self which does not change. It is our true self (not a material self).

609. **Q: What is Samsara?**

A: The chain of life that extends far into the past and projects far into the future. It is caused by lack of knowledge of our true self (spiritually).

610. **Q: What are the Hindus teaching?**

A: The teachings are in a text called Sutras or Aphorisms which Hindus are encouraged to memorise and recite to invoking or as a means of gaining spiritual focus.

611. **Q: What is karma?**

A: Our present condition in life is the consequence of the actions of our previous lives, i.e. your destiny.

612. **Q: What are Hindus Holy Books?**

A: Hindus have four important books called The Vedas (sacred literature) with separate titles. This is written in Sanskrit.

There are four Vedas which each are divided into four types of texts name: Mantra or Samhita, Brahmana, Aranyaka and Upanishad. There are no Holy books as there is no single revelation or orthodoxy for Hindu religion.

613. **Q: What are the names of Hindus scriptures?**

A: This is divided into two: Shuti and Smrili.

614. **Q: What is Ramayana of Valmiki?**

A: It is a book that describes the life of Prince Rama (an incarnation) of Vishnu. It is arguably the biggest book of text consisting of 24,000 verses.

615. **Q: What is Mahabharata?**

A: It is an epic story attributed to a sage named Vyasa. It has 100,000 verses and is the longest poem in the world.

616. **Q: Where do Hindus regard as sacred sites?**
A: The entire earth, as well as the Indian land mass known as mother India (Bharata Mata).

617. **Q: What is Puja?**
A: Devotion – worship daily deity individuals choose to worship.

618. **Q: What is Samskaras?**
A: This is sacraments to mark passages or the life cycle of the individual, e.g. the sacrament of death calls for creation.

619. **Q: What is "Om"?**
A: This is sacred verbal symbol and sacred sound. This is used when meditating on Brahman.

620. **Q: What is Guru?**
A: Teacher or Spiritual authority in Hinduism. It is someone who has attained realisation and acts as a guide for other human beings.

621. **Q: What do human beings consist of?**

A: Hindus believe human beings consist of five layers or sheaths called Koshas namely: Annamag (food or physical body), Pranamaya (energy), Manomaya (mind), Vijnanamaya (consciousness) and Anandamaya (bliss).

622. **Q: What is Yogas?**

A: This is the path to Brahman. It is believed that human personality is divided and dominated by a) physicality, b) activity, c) emotionally and d) intellectuality.

623. **Q: What is Hindu ritual?**

A: Hindus consider all of creation (on earth, sun and moon), worthy of worship but the head god is Parama or Supreme God that all religions worship.

All rituals in Hinduism have multiple meanings or interpretations due to the different branches and beliefs.

624. **Q: What is Bindi?**

A: This is the red dot that many women wear on their foreheads. It is a mark of good fortune.

625. **Q: Name other rituals.**

A: Three types of rituals are: *Yajna* (this involves sacrificial fire), *Puja* (devotional offerings – flowers) and *dhyana* (meditation). Human activities are divided into three: 1) *Nitya*: performed daily; 2) *Naimittika*: performed on specific occasions; and 3) *Kamya*: voluntary according to personal desire.

626. **Q: Name at least two festivals of Hindus.**

A: There are a few festivals which include Ganesh, Chathuthi, Mahasivarati, Holi, Ramnavami, Krishna, Janmastani and Magara Sankaranti. Holy festivals mark the arrival of spring in February/March.

Dassera (Navaralri or Durgapuja) festival marks the victory of Prince Rama over the demon king Ravana.

The most prominent festival is called Festival of Light or Diwali.

627. **Q: Describe the festival of light festival, "Diwali" Dussehra, Holi.**

A: 1. Diwali (or the festival of light to welcome the new year in October) where all houses hold lighted candles and put them on their windowsills. It is believed to welcome "Rama" (King God), the goddess of wealth (Lakshmi). During these times a lot of people, businesses and private, open new accounts.

2. Dussehra: A story being told acting Ramayana to celebrate good overcoming evil.

3. Holi: Usually India summer and it signifies joy and dedication to Krishna – all caste plays together, throwing water, powder and exchanging good wishes.

628. **Q: What is Satsanga?**

A: It is a fellowship keeping company with sat (truth and goodness). This is an occasion when Hindus gather for the discussion of the scripture.

629. **Q: How do you explain meditating in Hindus?**

A: Hindus chant the three syllable A...U...M as a means of meditating on the ultimate connecting the Atma (innermost self and Brahman). These mean manifestation, maintenance and dissolution.

Eshwara presides over Brahma, Vishnu and Shiva.

630. **Q: What is Ashrama?**

A: Human life is divided into four stages and four goals (Purusharthas): Dharma, Artha, Kama and Moksha.

631. **Q: What is Jiva?**

A: The individual personality influenced on the goal we seek.

632. **Q: What is Avatra?**

A: Avatra denotes "God has come from Heaven". It was believed that God came to the earth in a different form of Avatra in order to restore harmony on earth and to save mankind from destruction.

These beliefs of Avatra started when Noah built the Ark. The Indian religion believe God himself guided the boat safely onto Mount Avarat in Turkey.

Other Avatras are Rama and Krishna. According to India, they support the Bible

Revelation Chapter 19 about the prophesy of the last Avatar.

633. **Q: What do you think of Jesus Christ?**

A: The Hindus accept the contents of the Bible about Jesus Christ. They (Hindus, Krishna) believe just as Avatra (Lord Krishna, Rama) came to India before Jesus Christ, so Jesus being the son of God or God himself in Jesus came to give salvation to people. Also, that Jesus was a Divine Being who came to light the way that all religions followed him and joined him in full of God.

634. **Q: What do Hindus think of Muhammad?**

A: Hindus and Krishna fully endorse Prophet Muhammad as someone inspired by God himself to present God/Allah's word through the content of the Quran to all mankind not just Muslims.

The main content of the Quran, according to Hindus/Krishna, are similar to Veda, Bhagavad Gita (Hindus/Krishna – Holy book) and the Old Testament of the Holy Bible.

635. **Q: Do Hindus worship God?**

A: No.

636. **Q: Why do Hindus regard the cow as sacred?**

A: Cows provide a lot for humans and Hindus respect it as Samy's (God's) sacred creation.

637. **Q: How?**

A: Cows provide milk for both humans and animals for pets to feed on, the excretion (manure) can be used as fuel, this can also be mixed with mud (in correct proportions) as plaster for walls and floors.

The male cow (bull) can be used for travelling (carry goods and to plough the fields).

The text Vedic regard cows as divine of the world. These beliefs play major parts in Hindu scriptum, hence they have strong respect for cows, they do not eat or kill them, and they definitely do not eat beef. This is one of the reasons why most Hindus are vegetarians.

638. **Q: What is the significance of river Ganges?**

A: It is sacred and every year, Hindus take a pilgrimage to bath in it naked (both sexes).

639. **Q: What is mandir?**

A: It is the name for the Hindu temple or worship place.

640. **Q: What is so important of mandir?**

A: It is where the mind is the centre for realising God and the mind become motionless. Through meditation in mandir one can obtain the highest peace because it stimulates higher wisdom in life. It teaches humans to love and respect one another.

By Pujya Pramukh Swami Maharaj (b.1921)

641. **Q: Name the major Yoga.**

A: Karma Yoga, Jnana yoga, Raja yoga, Mantra yoga and Bhakti yoga.

642. **Q: What do they mean?**

A: Karma yoga is where the mind is fixed on God (Brahma).

Raja yoga is how one controls the mind to stop it is wandering.

Bhakti is whereby one meditates on a specific image to God.

Mantra yoga worshipping/devotion to God.

Jnana yoga is knowledge acquired through study.

643. **Q: What is shrutis?**

A: This is regarded as the oldest Vedas book.

644. **Q: Name some Vedas and give a brief meaning.**

A: Atharva Veda – science knowledge

Sama Veda – worshipping knowledge

Yajur Veda – action knowledge

Rig Veda – is the longest of the Vedas as it provides general knowledge.

645. **Q: Name the three main Hindu Gods.**

A: 1. The Creator (Brahma); 2. The Preserver (Vishnu); 3. The Destroyer (Shiva).

646. **Q: What is an "avatar"?**

A: An avatar is an incarnation in that God himself discerns to earth when the evil of men increases.

647. **Q: Name some Avatars.**

A: Krishna, Vishm, Brahma, Shiva, Ganesh (remover of obstacles) or the elephant head, Lakshmi (fortune and beauty), Kali, Shiva consort (cease war and illness), Parvati and Durg, and Hanunma – God of monkey.

648. **Q: What is a Caste system?**

A: It is a system in India dating back centuries where the same group members marry themselves and have its own traditional occupation, diet, rules, myths and forms of behaviour.

649. **Q: What is the origin of Caste?**

A: Caste is also known as verma (it means colour). It is very important in India and determines one's social life: marriage, economic status.

650. **Q: How many castes are there and name them?**

A: There are four main castes from which there are other sub-divisions:

1st: Brahmins – are the priesthood class

2nd: Kshatriyas – Are the warriors and ruler class

3rd: Vaishya's – Are the farmers and commercial class

4th: Shudras – Are the artisans and servant class.

651. **Q: What is the untouchable class?**

A: This is not part of the class, it could be those higher than Brahmins; they are very self-sufficient.

652. **Q: What is Divine Light Mission?**

A: It is a special meditation consisting of four techniques and is aimed for self-understanding and communion with the inner soul, which is described as music, nectar Holy name Divine Light (Elan Vital).

653. **Q: What is Bhagavad Gita?**

A: This is the Hindu holy philosophy which contains God's word.

654. **Q: What is the process of Hindu weddings?**

A: Hindus concept of marriage is between two families as well as two individuals and so it is arranged by the parents.

655. **Q: What are Hindus' sacred text?**

A: There are two main types of Sacred Texts:

1. Shruti (means head) written in Vedas and describes the word of God.

2.   Smiritti (means remembered) the authors of Sages, e.g. Ramayana and Mahabharata.

656.   **Q: Which is the oldest and newest sacred text?**

A: Vedas is divided into four which is the oldest or the most ancient.

The most sacred is the earliest and regarded as the most sacred.

657.   **Q: Which text is Brahman?**

A: Upanishads is the philosophy descried as Vedanta and is specially for Brahman also known as World Soul.

658.   **Q: Which Hindu text was written between 300BCE and 300CE?**

A: Mahabharata, which is written in a stony form consists especially of civil wars and fights between good and evil.

659.   **Q: What is the Bhargavad Gita?**

A: This is the best known, earliest song of the Lord containing a spiritual poem, about Lord god Krishna and Prince Arjuna. Hindus believe that the God Brahman was incarnated as Lord Krishna.

660. **Q: Is there any other text containing poems?**
A: Yes, it is called Ramayana, which is a story of Lord Rama fighting and rescuing his wife (Sita) from King Ravana (demon).

661. **Q: Name some beliefs of Hindus.**
A: Hindus believe in reincarnation in that even though the body dies, the soul is reborn.

662. **Q: What will be the characteristic of the newly reborn?**
A: The reincarnation will have the same status as the previous, i.e. if one does good then the soul comes back too as a good being.

663. **Q: What is this circle of reincarnation?**
A: Hindus share this circle with Buddhism and it is called "Karma".

664. **Q: When does this reincarnation stop?**
A: Well, for the soul to be accepted by the God of Brahman, it has to leave the life and be rebirthed, known as Samsara and to gain freedom known as moksha.

665. **Q: It appears the ultimate goal is to achieve freedom (moksha). How does one gain this?**

A: There are three ways called paths:

1. By meditation, ascetic and yoga, one can obtain knowledge.

2. The other way (path) is the soul's good works and to fulfil all social and spiritual obligations.

3. The third way is by devotion or "bhakti".

666. **Q: What do Hindus aim for?**

A: They aim for Nirguna Brahman or Absolute which then leads to salvation (being God's gift).

667. **Q: Name two elaborate Hindu temples.**

A: Hindu temple in Delhi and Siv Mandir temple in Varanasi (Holy cities).

668. **Q: Describe an example of the Hindu God.**

A: The God of Ganesh has four hands, one holding a rosary, one a snake, one a tusk and the fourth is used to bless devotees. He is the son of God of destroyer (Shiva). Ganesh is alleged to have control over death.

669. **Q: Where did Hinduism and its name originate?**

A: India used to be called Sanatana Dharma, which means perennial righteous conduct.

670. **Q: What do Hindus believe in?**

A: In one God or Goddess.

671. **Q: What is Hindus' view on the soul?**

A: That the human soul/animal soul is divine and immortal, that the soul remains independent of the body, hence the soul retains its purity.

672. **Q: What qualities are expected from Hindus?**

A: These include non-violence, respect to all faiths, mercy to all creatures known as Kshama, human action must be pure or clean, including the mind and the spirit known as shuchi, forgiveness, generosity, love your enemies, restrain desire, greed, truthfulness and be simple (known as Jnana and Vairagya).

673. **Q: Name a few of the Hindus main festivals.**

A:

1. Maha Shivaratri (one day fasting), the God Shiva is worshipped all night (one day in March).

2. Rakhee/Raksha Bandham (in August) is a family get-together – brothers and sisters.

3. Shri-Ganesha Pooja (August–September) celebrates Lord Ganesh.

4. Shri-Krishna Jan Ashtami (one at midnight in August) to celebrate Lord Krishna's birthday.

5. Diwali: the festival of lights and to welcome in the new year (usually in November).

6. Vijayada shami/Dasha Hara: This marks the end of Navaratri.

7. Makara Sankramang or Sankranti or Uttarayana Punkayala.

8. Holi – the festival of colours to welcome the coming of spring (March).

9. Yugadi/Gudi Parva.

10. Baisakhi (April) in Punjabi.

11. Shri Rama Navami – where by day (March or April) they worship Lord Rama.

12. Guru Purnima: Shraddha Paksha, Navaratri (in October).

13. Durgashtami.

674. **Q: Are there any restrictions on diet?**

A: The majority of Hindus are vegetarians and they refrain from eating meat, fish, eggs or any food containing eggs. The minority who eat meat and fish avoid beef and pork. No alcohol and no tobacco is allowed.

675. **Q: What titles are used in Hindu?**

A: Hindus do not use Mr, Mrs or Miss, instead they use:

- Shri for Mr, e.g. Shri Patel.
- Shrimati for Mrs, e.g. Shrimati Patel.
- Sush or Kumari for Miss, e.g. Sush Patel.

676. **Q: What happens when death occurs?**

A: The family mourns for ten days including fasting for the closest family before cremation (other ceremonies take place at the same time).

677. **Q: What rituals are there when Hindus are dying?**

A: The dying person lies on the floor as a sign of respect and close to the earth and somebody reads the portion from the Bhagavad-Gita. The Hindu priest is then called to officiate the last (holy) rites.

678. **Q: How is the Hindu prepared for burial?**

A: You must not remove any jewels or religious objects from the dead body. Wrapping sheets should not contain any religious marks. A relative usually washes the dead body. Most Hindus are cremated and the eldest son presses the ignition button at the cremation.

679. **Q: How does a marriage take place?**

A: First by a registrar, then the other ceremony takes place in the local hall for the reception.

680. **Q: What did Lord Krishna say about Austerities of the mind?**

A: The existence of satisfaction, simplicity, gravity, self-control and purification.

681. **Q: What is the mode of goodness?**

A: To give to charity and not expect a reward at any time.

682. **Q: What did Lord Krishna say about the mode of ignorance?**

A: To give to charity at an impure place or improper time to unworthy people or without proper attention and respect.

683. **Q: What is the absolute truth?**

A: It is the objective of devotional sacrifice and it is indicated by the word "sat" which means "the performance of such charity".

684. **Q: According to the modes what are the three foods?**

A: Foods of goodness increases the duration of life, purifies one's existence and gives strength, health, happiness and satisfaction.

685. **Q: Describe the food of goodness.**

A: Juicy, fatty, wholesome and pleasing to the heart.

686. **Q: What are the foods of passion?**

A: They are bitter, too sour, salty, hot, pungent, dry and burning.

687. **Q: What do foods of passion cause?**

A: Distress, misery and disease.

688. **Q: What sort of foods are preferred by those in darkness?**

A: Food eaten more than three hours after preparation, which is tasteless, consisting of remnants and is decomposing.

689. **Q: What are the five factors of action?**

A: The body (place of action), the performer, the various senses, different kinds of endeavour and ultimately the super soul.

690. **Q: What do these factors do?**

A: When the main body, mind or speech relates to right or wrong.

691. **Q: What did Krishna say about faults?**

A: Every endeavour has some faults; therefore, one should not give up the work born of his nature.

692. **Q: What human reaction can give the highest stage of freedom?**

A: One who is self-controlled, unattached, disregards all material enjoyments by practice of renunciation.

693. **Q: Who was Lord Krishna?**

A: He was the supreme truth, the supreme cause and sustaining force of everything both material and spiritual, supreme Godhead.

694. **Q: Who is the one who attains liberation from the material world?**

A: Anyone who knows the difference between the body, the soul and the super soul.

695. **Q: What did Krishna say relates to God?**

A: Never was there a time when I did not exist, nor you, nor all these kings, nor in the future shall any of us cease to be.

696. **Q: What did Lord Krishna say which related to God?**

A: "The whole cosmic order is under Me. Under my will it is automatically manifested again and again, and under My will it is annihilated at the end.

"I am the goal, the sustainer, the master, the witness, the abode, the refuge and the most dear friend, I am the creation and the annihilation, the basis of everything, the resting place and the eternal seed.

"I give heat and withhold and send forth the rain. I am immortality and I am also death personified. Both spirit and matter are in me.

"I am the father of this universe, the mother, the support and the grandsire. I am the object of knowledge, the purifier and the syllable.

"I am the only enjoyer and master of all sacrifice. Therefore, those who do not recognise my true transcendental nature falls down.

"Of purifiers, I am the wind, of the wielders of weapons, I am Rama, of fishes I am the shark and of flowing rivers I am Ganges."

Lord Krishna is everything, a letter, him, gambling cheat, source of light in all luminous knowledge, object of knowledge, God of knowledge and he is situated in everyone's heart.

697. **Q: How many gates lead to Hell?**
A: Lust, anger and greed. You must give these up.

698. **Q: Who does Lord Krishna call a pretender?**
A: One who restrains their sense of actions, but whose mind dwells on sense objects certainly deludes himself.

699. **Q: Who is superior in the eyes of Lord Krishna?**

A: One who is a sincere person and tries to control their active senses by the mind and begins Karma Yoga without attachment.

700. **Q: What did Lord Krishna say about work?**

A: Perform your prescribed duty for doing so is better than not working. One cannot even maintain one's physical body without work.

701. **Q: What did he say about great men?**

A: Whatever action a great man performs, common men follow. And whatever standards he sets by exemplary acts all the world pursues.

702. **Q: Where does one find faith?**

A: The mind, the senses and the intelligence.

703. **Q: What did Krishna say about intelligence, etc.?**

A: The working senses are superior to dull matter; minds are higher than the senses, intelligence is still higher than the mind and the soul is even higher than the intelligence.

704. **Q: What did Lord Krishna say about fruitive activities?**

A: Those who desire success in fruitive activities and therefore they worship the demigods and quickly get results.

705. **Q: How did Lord Krishna describe himself?**

A: I am the original fragrance of the earth and I am the heat in fire, I am the life of all that lives, and I am the penances of all ascetics.

706. **Q: What is Krishna's meaning of Atma?**

A: Human beings or Atma consist of spirit that remains the same throughout life, but the body which is matter changes from a baby, grows old and then dies.

When one dies the Atma (spirit) leaves the body so that when you touch a dead body, you cannot have any feelings because the Atma or spirit that controls it had left.

In short Atma is a spirit within flesh and bone eternal, knowledgeable and blissful.

707. **Q: According to Krishna what does our body consist of?**

A: Krishna followers believe that the body consists of two parts: the gross or physical body that we can see and touch and the subtle body consists of mind, intelligence and ego.

708. **Q: What are the types of ego?**

A: Real ego which we use to identify ourselves as Atma.

False ego: this is when one thinks of the body.

709. **Q: What are Vedas?**

A: They are the oldest books of knowledge in Hindus – India. It has four main headings namely medical technology, the ideals of family life, social law, statecraft and religious practice.

710. **Q: Who wrote the Vedas and the Bhagavad Gita?**

A: These Hindus and Vaishnava (Krishna followers) were believed to have been written by Vyasa Deva who was a reincarnation of Krishna.

711. **Q: When and who started Vaishnava religion?**

A: It was started about 500 years ago by Chitanya Maha Prabhu.

712. **Q: What is the name of their worship place?**

A: The worship building is called Mandir and no specific day is allocated for worship.

713. **Q: What qualifies one to be a Vaishnava?**

First one needs a Guru or teacher.

714. **Q: What are their beliefs?**

A: That Atma is the spiritual or the soul of humans which existed before and after the body (living entity).

They also believe in reincarnation of the soul which means when one dies the soul comes back as somebody else.

They also believe in Calma (Action) which means you harvest what you sow.

Hence when you die you will be rewarded if you have done good and be punished if you have done bad.

715. **Q: Why does Hinduism have a caste status system?**

A: The Hindus have ancient code which is known as the Laws of Manu. These determine the behaviour (socially) and obligations of the four classes and they must be followed to live in accordance with Dharma.

716. **Q: What is the significance of the code system?**

A: The code gives characteristics which lead each Hindu from birth to death and rebirth. It offers guidance on all issues including marriage, hospitality, dietary restrictions and religious duties.

These codes or scriptures are traditionally attributed to Svayambhuva in, i.e. Hindu legend the first ancestor.

717. **Q: Describe Moksha?**

A: If Hindus reach spirituality attainment called *Moksha* the enlightenment can occur to any Hindus regardless of their caste status and upon the life lived by an individual. It is believed that the person's soul will be promoted or demoted, by being born again into a higher or lower status caste. Moksha is the ultimate aim of all Hindus human life. It is characterised by liberation from sorrow and desire and realisation of the union with the ultimate reality which is known as the Brahman. When somebody is born Hindus consider it as a unique and valuable opportunity for seeking Moksha which must not be wasted.

718. **Q: What other paths are there to attain Moksha?**

A: There are several paths open for Hindus to achieve the Moksha state: concentration on Brahman, a life of solitary meditation and encompassing the discipline of yoga. To attain Moksha is freedom from the world and from desires for Kama, Artha and Dharma. It is an extraordinary goal and only a few special people achieve this.

719. **Q: What is Hindus' interpretation of human life and describe the four main stages?**

A: Hindus believe there are four stages of life with its own characteristics (Dharma).

The first stage is childhood with dominant emphasis on education.

The second stage is household which focuses on bringing up a successful family.

The third stage is retirement or becoming a grandparent. This stage concentrates closely on spiritual matters.

The fourth and final stage is the end of life when he/she becomes devout by renouncing the world and concentrating on the absolute.

Chapter 7

Islam

720. **Q: What does Islam mean?**

A: Peace and submission.

721. **Q: What is the name of one who submits to the creator?**

A: A Muslim. Who worship Allah through Allah.

722. **Q: What is Islam main belief?**

A: Unity of Oneness of Allah (God).

723. **Q: What else do Muslims believe?**

A: All the major prophets in the Old Testament and Jesus in the New Testament as the Messiah's son of Mary. They also believe that Muhammad was the last prophet of God/Allah to who was revealed the Holy words of the Quran.

724. **Q: Who else do they believe God revealed his word to?**

A: The Ten Commandments to Moses, Psalms to David, New Testament to Jesus and the Quran to Prophet Muhammad.

725. **Q: What are the main sources of Muslim teaching?**

A: The Quran, Hadith or Sunnah.

726. **Q: What are the five principle/practice/Pillars of the Islam faith?**

A:

a. Shahadah: declaration of faith.

b. Salah: five prayers a day.

c. Sawn: Ramadan fasting.

d. Zakah: contribution of individual finance supposed to be given to the poor and needy.

e. Hajj: pilgrimage to Makkah.

727. **Q: What do they believe about humans?**

A: That the angel recorded every action of humans and the results were presented on Judgement day.

728. **Q: What is the aim of Islam or the Muslims?**

A: To worship God, do good, love his creation, prevent harm, pray for God's grace on earth and the afterlife.

729. **Q: What is Jumuah?**

A: This is Friday noon worship which is compulsory.

730. **Q: Which direction do Muslim prayers face?**

A: They face in the direction of Makkah.

731. **Q: What are Ablutions?**

A: This is the ritual of washing before prayers which is obligatory.

732. **Q: What about their diet?**

A: They are only to eat Halal food which is food permissible under Islamic law.

733. **Q: Name a few festivals.**

A: Ramadan – fasting (no food, drink or sex from morning 6a.m. to 6p.m. for 40 days).

734. **Q: What is Eid-ul and Eid-ul-Adha?**

A: This involves the arrangement for various things such as communal feasts, prayers, fasting and phone calls.

735. **Q: What is Eid-ul-Fitr?**

A: Celebration after Ramadan.

736. **Q: What is Eid-ul-Adha?**

A: To remember when Prophet Ibrahim's accepted God's command to sacrifice his son Ismael.

737. **Q: What is Milad an-Nabi?**

A: The celebration of the birthday of Prophet Muhammad.

738. **Q: What is Ashurg?**

A: To mark the celebration of Prophet Muhammad and his disciples' freedom from tyranny of King Pharaoh. Also, the martyrdom of Iman Hussain "grandson of Prophet Muhammad".

739. **Q: Why do Muslims always say Peace Be Upon Him (PBUH) when they mention Prophet Muhammad?**

A: It is a sign of utmost respect.

740. **Q: What is The Day of Hijrah?**

A: Muslims New Year (when Prophet Muhammad migrated from Makkah to Medina).

741. **Q: What is Muharran?**

A: The tenth day of the first month in the Islamic Calendar.

742. **Q: What is Al-Isra wa al-Miray?**

A: This is known as the Ascension to Heaven by Prophet Muhammad (PBUH) on 17 [th] of Rajab.

743. **Q: What is Laylat Ul-Qadr?**

A: On 27th of Ramadan known as Night of power (the last of ten nights of Ramadan).

744. **Q: How do women dress?**

A: They have a choice of either a headscarf (hijab) or they wear veils.

745. **Q: What clothes do men wear?**

A: There are no restrictions, but they are to avoid nakedness from the umbilical cord to the knees.

746. **Q: What special things do Muslims do when fasting?**

A: They shave pubic and underarm hair and clip fingernails and toenails within 40 days.

747. **Q: What about marriage?**

A: The Imam officiates the religious marriage and this is followed by a civil marriage.

748. **Q: What happens when Muslims die?**

A: All Muslims are buried; cremation is forbidden.

749. **Q: What are the two main teachings in Islam?**

A: Sunni school and Shia Muslim.

750. **Q: How would you describe Sunni?**

A: There is not much difference.

751. **Q: How would you describe the Shia Muslims?**

A: They differ in that Imam Ali, the son-in-law and Prophet Muhammad's cousin succeeded him. Abi was the first of the 12 who succeeded Prophet Muhammad. They both agree Prophet Muhammad was the last of God/Allah's Messengers, is Holy Quran, the same as prayers, fasting, Haji, Zakat and Shia Muslim's commemorate Ashura.

752. **Q: How long did it take for the Quran to be revealed to Prophet Muhammad?**

A: 23 years.

753. **Q: Where was it revealed and by whom?**

A: In a cave by Arch Angel Gabriel.

754. **Q: How many prophets were there before prophet Muhammad?**

A: 16–20.

755. **Q: Name some.**

A: Ibrahim, Adam, Isaac, Ismael, Job, Joseph, Isaiah, Jeremiah, Job and David.

756. **Q: What is the Quran?**

A: It is a Holy Book that contains the words of Allah with guidance and direction for the whole of mankind. It teaches human beings that they were created to worship Allah that true-worship is God-consciousness.

Bernard Shaw wrote: "If a man like Muhammad were to assume the dictatorship of the modern word, he would succeed in solving its problems… and in my opinion far from being an anti-Christ he must be called the saviour of humanity."

757. **Q: Why do the interpretations of the Quran contain slight meanings?**

A: Because there are different Muslim groups of languages, hence it depends on the interpreter's background.

758. **Q: Initially how many times did God ask Muslims to pray before reducing it to five times a day?**

A: 50.

759. **Q: How many chapters are there in the Quran?**

A: 114.

760. **Q: How many verses are there in the Quran?**

A: Over 6,000.

761. **Q: How many verses did the Arch Angel Gabriel reveal to Prophet Muhammad the first time?**

A: Five verses.

762. **Q: Did Prophet Muhammad ever meet Allah?**

A: It is believed so.

763. **Q: What might one consider when reading the Quran?**

A: It is important to bear in mind that the Quran was revealed over 23 years, hence it depended what was happening at the time, the reason of the revelation and the history behind it.

764. **Q: Is it possible that some of the way of life is no longer necessary?**

A: According to the Quran and my research, Allah knows and sees beyond. Therefore, the content of the Quran is forever until Judgement day.

765. **Q: What is the meaning of Muhammad?**

My Prophet, my hero – my hand to hold

Unlettered, unrivalled, benevolent and bold

Honour and respect, I duly uphold

A man whose life, they tried to scold

My rock to lean on, my castle of old

Messengers of Allah, to their nations foretold

A final prophet, within their fold

Decorated the world, with Character of Gold.

766. **Q: Who is All-compassionate, All-Merciful, All-Knowing?**

A: Allah/God/Sammy.

767. **Q: What causes human problems?**

A: Anger, arrogance, greed, cheating, live by today and not accept life after death, hatred, jealousy, envy, OTT (over the top) by excessiveness, doing things to show off, worshiping idols, evil spirit, rulers of darkness, underworld, no compassion for the needy, hatred, ignorance, not being patient for Allah/God/Sammy to answer your supplication, lack of justice, not being grateful, hypocrite, selfishness, judge people on other faiths, power seeking, unable to discipline oneself, lack of motivation, laziness and relationships.

768. **Q: How does one prevent problems?**

A: Reflect and accept you have problems.

Pray to Allah/God/Sammy by fasting and follow the mode of worshipping.

Repent to God/Allah/Sammy.

Mix with people of good character, especially those with good faiths. Make a list of both physical and psychological plans. Attend God's house regularly.

769. **Q: Name the part of the physical body that commits or solves problems?**

A: Eyes, ears, tongue, feet, hands, stomach and private parts.

770. **Q: What do Muslims believe (all sections of Islam)?**

A: All Muslims with no exception believe in:

There is only one Allah.

That Allah sent his prophets as Messengers and Warners to every nation and tribe/culture to teach them to benefit from their time on earth and to live in harmony with his creation, that He revealed His final book "Quran" to his final messenger Muhammad Ref. al-Insan al-Kamil the perfect man.

771. **What do Muslims accept without exception?**

A: Life after death.

There will be a judgement day.

Allah's creation consists of seen and unseen.

All Muslims believe their practice is right despite difference in interpretation.

772. **Q: What are the main obligations of Muslims?**

A: To face the direction of Makkah and worship Allah five times a day.

Too fast for the month of Ramadan.

To pay their religious dues.

If they are able, to go on a pilgrimage (haji) once in their lifetime.

773. **Q: Name the three branches of Islam.**

A:

a. Shi'a.

b. Sunni.

c. Sunfish.

774. **Q: Why is Makkah not dangerous?**

A: Because prophets said no one can carry weapons.

775. **Q: What verse relates to light, David, Solomon and moral.**

A: Allah is the light of Heaven and earth, Allah light analogous to a lamp in a niche in glass to appear as a shining star. Quran 24:38.

Truly we graced David as "O mountains sing our praise with him. We made subservient to Solomon, the wind which covers a month's journey in a morning." Quran 34:10, 12.

You must not worship any other Gods except Allah, do not reproach, behave irritably or reject them, but always respond gently, treat them with humanity, with tenderness, praying, "Allah be merciful to them as they were to me when I was little."

Allah is aware of what is in your heart and how you behave. He is All-forgiving to those who repent... Quran 17:23–29.

776. **Q: What is the difference between Islam and Muslim?**

A: Islam is an Arabic word meaning submitting and surrendering your will to Almighty God (Allah). Muslims are those who submit themselves totally to Allah and attain true peace.

777. **Q: Why do Muslims say peace be with you (SWT)?**

A: They say this when Muhammad's name is mentioned as he was the holiest, most honest, most respected and God messenger and the last prophet of Allah.

778. **Q: Who is Allah?**

A: It can be explained with two parts. Al = which is the definitive article in Arabic and Allah is an object to which subservience Allah signifies one and only supreme deity and one to whom absolute love, reverence and obedience is given.

779. **Q: What are the teachings of Islam?**

A: It is to have faith and believe that there is only one creator and sustained of everything in the Universe and that nothing is divine or worthy of being worshipped except Allah. And the way of life is full of justice, equality, universal, brotherhood and peace.

780. **Q: Who was the first Islam person to be circumcised?**

A: Abraham/Ibrahim

781. **Q: Who was the first person to introduce fasting for three days a month?**

A: Adam.

782. **Q: Who was the first Prophet of Israel?**

A: Moses, he led the Israelites from the slavery.

783. **Q: Which Prophet was the first human to be affected by smallpox?**

A: Job.

784. **Q: According to Islam who was the first astrologist?**

A: Noah.

785.   Q: **Who built the first building in which to worship God and what name was given to it?**

A: Adam built it and it was called the Ka'ba.

786.   Q: **What was the first thing that the angel Gabriel taught Muhammad (S.A.W)?**

A: How to perform ablution, the first time the Arch angel appear to Muhammed he was commanded to read and then the first few verses of the Quran were revealed to him

787.   Q: **What was the first religious duty ordained by God for the Islamic community?**

A: To seek knowledge.

788.   Q: **Who was the first adult male to accept Islam?**

A: Abu Bakr Siddique, who was the prophet's companion.

789.   Q: **Who was the first child to accept the message of Islam?**

A: Ali ibn Abu Talib.

790.   Q: **Who was the first woman to enter Islam?**

A: Khadija, the wife of Muhammad (S.A.W).

791. **Q: Who was the first negro slave to enter Islam?**

A: Bilal. He was also the first to black Muslim to call for prayers.

792. **Q: Who were the first three people to publicly announce the reversion to Islam?**

A: Muhammad (S.A.W), Abu Bakr and Bilal.

793. **Q: Who was the first person to make the call to prayer for all the Muslims?**

A: Bilal, he had a beautiful voice. Some Arabs complained because his pronunciation was not perfect.

794. **Q: Who was the first person to pray for Muhammad (S.A.W) after his passing?**

A: His uncle, al-Abbas ibn Abd al-Muttalib.

795. **Q: Who led the first Islamic army from Madinah after the passing of Muhammad (S.A.W)?**

A: Usamah.

796. **Q: Who was the first caliph after Muhammad (S.A.W)?**

A: Abu Bakr Siddique. Followed by Umar ibn al-Khattab, then Uthman and then Ali ibn Abu Talib.

797. **Q: Who was caliph when it was decided to compile the Quran into one ledger?**
A: Abu Bakr.

798. **Q: Who was the Islamic leader to import food from Egypt via the Gulf of Aqabah?**
A: Umar al-Farooq.

799. **Q: Who was the first caliph to initiate conquests outside of the Arabian Peninsula?**
A: Umar al-Farooq.

800. **Q: Who was the first caliph to establish garrison towns, for Muslims?**
A: Umar al-Farooq.

801. **Q: Name the garrison towns first established.**
A: Kufah, Basra, al-Jazirah, Mawsi, as-Sham and Fustat.

802. **Q: Who was the first Islamic governor of Egypt?**
A: Amr bin al-Aas.

803. **Q: Who was the first person to appoint a police chief?**

A: Uthman.

804. **Q: Who was the first person to unite the Muslims under one dialect for worship, after Muhammad (S.A.W)?**

A: Uthman ibn Uffan.

805. **Q: Which caliph built the first prison in the Islamic period?**

A: Ali ibn Abu Talib.

806. **Q: Before the construction of prisons how did the righteous deal with criminals?**

A: They would be detained in dungeons or dried up wells. (Abar, reference Suyuti, op.cit. p.84).

807. **Q: Who was the first person to embellish mosques in Madinah and Damascus?**

A: AlWalid bin Abd al-Malik, he was also the first person to order purpose-built hospitals.

808. **Q: What is Islam?**

A: Islam means peace or submission to the will of God. It teaches belief in the Oneness of God, Judgement Day and personal accountability for one's own actions.

809. **Q: What are the basic beliefs of Muslims?**

A: There are seven articles of faith, upon which Islam is built, which have a similar standing to the "Nicene Creed". They are as follows:

Allah (S.W.T): Belief in Allah (S.W.T), God. There is only one God with no associate or partners. The past, present and future are all controlled by the omnipotent, supreme, being.

Angels: Angels are created from light and execute the commands of Allah (S.W.T) without question or choice. They are not given free will, as humans are. Some are mentioned by name within the Quran and hadith. Jibra'eel (Gabriel), Mika'eel (Michael), Israfeel, Isra'eel, Malik, Munkir and Ankir. They each have specific duties assigned by Allah (S.W.T).

The books of Allah (S.W.T): There are four scriptures mentioned in the Quran. The Psalms (Zaboor) of David, the Torah (Taurat) of Moses, The Gospel (Injeel) of Jesus and the Quran itself. The Injeel is not the Bible, but the Gospel revealed to Jesus.

The Prophets: There have been many thousands of Prophets sent by Allah (S.W.T) to humanity. If they taught monotheism, then Muslims accepted them. Between Adam and Muhammad (S.A.W) the exact number of Prophets was known only to Allah (S.W.T). However, in an authentic hadith Muhammad (S.A.W) was quoted as having said there were at least 124,000 before him. And Muhammad (S.A.W) was the last of that line. There are 25 mentioned by name in the Quran, they are: Adam, Enoch, Noah, Abraham, Lot, Ishmael, Isaac, Jacob, Joseph, Job, Moses, Aaron, King David, King Solomon, Jonah, Zachariah, John (the Baptist) and Jesus are just some of them.

Day of Judgement: The day when all of creation will be raised, brought to account and judged for their deeds, good and bad.

Divine Decree: Allah's (S.W.T) pre-ordainment of all things that happen from the rising of the sun, to the death of an ant. Nothing happens without the will of Allah (S.W.T).

Life After Death: An afterlife where one will reap the rewards or punishments for their actions during this mortal lifetime.

To state a declaration of faith is to say one believes in all these things without question. Disbelief or non-acceptance of one of these articles take one out of the fold of Islam.

810. **Q: How do Muslims show their obedience to Allah (S.W.T)?**

A: There are five separate things that a Muslim is obligated to perform throughout their lives. Not performing these acts will be counted as sins. They are as follows:

Shahaada (Declaration of Faith). To be a Muslim one must testify, in front of witnesses, that they believe there is only one God and Muhammad (S.A.W) is His Messenger. The words spoken for this in Arab are: *La illaha illullah, Muhammadan Rasoolullah.*

Salaat (Prayer). Every day there are five obligatory prescribed times that a Muslim must pray. They correspond to the arc of the sun so are at different times each day. The only times that Muslims are not allowed to pray are at the rising of the sun, the setting of the sun and when the sun reaches its zenith.

Zakaat (Charity). Each year a portion of one's wealth (2.5%), must be paid to a worthy charity. This is only calculated on static funds over a set amount.

Sawm (Fasting). To observe the rules of fasting during the ninth Islamic month Ramadan.

Hajj (Pilgrimage). To visit Mecca and perform the pilgrimage rites once during one's lifetime, if financially and physically able. If one is not physically able then it is acceptable to fund somebody else to complete this act upon your behalf.

811. **Q: Why do Muslims pray five times a day?**

A: First and foremost: Because we were commanded to by Allah (S.W.T). Five dailies prayers are obligatory; a vast number of people perform more! Anyone who practices prayers, in any religion, is aware of the benefits of prayer.

The ability to focus on and speak to God, no matter what is going on around us is incomparable to anything else.

812. **Q: Why do you wash to pray?**

A: As with the previous answer, primarily because we are told to. Also, this has two parts to it, spiritual and physical: spiritually the ablutions wash away minor sins accumulated since the last time. Physically, it is hygienic. You will rarely find a Muslim with smelly feet!

813. **Q: Why do you pray to the east?**

A: The direction of prayer is not the East. From Britain Muslims face south east, but the focal point or the direction of prayer, is towards the holy Ka'ba, in Mecca, on the Arabian Peninsula. All Muslims face the Ka'ba during all prayers.

814. **Q: Do Muslims worship Muhammad (S.A.W)?**

A: No! That is the reason we are not "Muhammadins". The greatest sin in Islam is to worship anything or anyone, other than Allah (S.W.T). Muhammad (S.A.W) is held in the highest esteem and acknowledged as the greatest of Allahs' (S.W.T) creations, but not worshipped.

815. **Q: I was surprised that you believe in Jesus and Mary?**

A: Muslims are obligated to believe in all the Prophets that taught monotheism. Jesus is one of the five great messengers and exalted amongst mankind. Mary has the honorific title of "Greatest of All Women". In the Quran there is a surah named after her and hers is the only female name explicitly revealed in the Quran.

816. **Q: I was also surprised that you believe in Moses. I thought he was just for the Jews and that there was enmity between Jews and Muslims?**

A: Moses was a Prophet of Allah (S.W.T) who was sent to the children of Israel, who consisted of both the Jews and the Arabs. He was sent to save them from the persecution at the hands of Pharaoh in Egypt and to guide them back to the truth of monotheism. He (Moses) was a Muslim. He taught belief in One God, no partners. He also instructed prayers, fasting and the payment of charity. We believe in all Prophets equally without discrimination. As for the belief that Muslims hate the Jews, that was brought about partly by the Middle Eastern conflict, mainly in Palestine/Israel. Medi influenced propaganda that even some Muslims believe. Both Christians and Jews are to be respected and anyone who claims to be a Muslim should know that Muhammad (S.A.W) married a Jew and a Christian woman. Their names were Safiya and Maria respectively. Both, through their marriage to Muhamad (S.A.W), earned the honorific title "Mother of the Believers".

817. **Q: It was said that Muhammad (S.A.W) was the last Prophet. How do you know this?**

A: Don't you think that we need a new up-to-date Prophet for modern society?

Yes, Muhammad (S.A.W) was the Last Prophet and the last Messenger, for the whole Universe. If his teachings had been lost or corrupted, as they were with Jesus and Moses, then a new Prophet may have been needed. However, it is globally accepted that the Quran is still authentic and intact in its original totality. Each of the Prophets before Muhammad (S.A.W) were sent to a specific people, region or time. Muhammad (S.A.W) was sent for the entire creation and in the Quran there are guidance for mankind. Allah (S.W.T) was very specific in His commands and spoke separately to unbelievers, pious believers and to all of mankind. The Quran is Allah's (S.W.T) testament.

818. **Q: Christians have the concept of original sin. Where does Islam stand on this?**

A: In Islam every person is born pure, without sin. Allah (S.W.T) is merciful and to suggest that he burdened us prior to our birth, with sins, is to doubt His mercy. Allah (S.W.T) made us pure as crystal ice, when we reach puberty we become accountable for all our deeds, which are preceded by intention. Because we are born free of sin we don't need to be baptised.

819. **Q: I thought Allah (S.W.T) was a black/Asian God?**

A: This is a common misconception. Allah (S.W.T) is God as already explained. There is no caste system in Islam. Muhammad (S.A.W) passed on the words of Allah (S.W.T) and in his final sermon said about racism and that Arabs have no superiority over non-Arabs, blacks over whites, whites over blacks or non-Arabs over Arabs. The only way to judge amongst mankind is in knowledge. All other judgements should be left for Allah (S.W.T).

820. **Q: If Muslims believe in Jesus why don't they celebrate Christmas?**

A: Muslims believe in the Prophet Jesus. He was one of the "Five Mighty Messengers", of Allah (S.W.T). However, Muslims do not celebrate the birth of any Prophet. The Prophets themselves did not celebrate their own birthdays. And anyway, the origins of Christmas lie in the pagan/Roman celebration of the winter solstice. This was adopted by Emperor Constantine when he created Roman Catholicism as a state religion.

821. **Q: Does Islam consider Christians and Jews as believers?**

A: They are mentioned in the Quran as "Children of the Book" meaning their origins lie in the scriptures revealed by Allah (S.W.T). However, these scriptures have been distorted by human hands. The people who followed Moses were believers, when Jesus came: the people who followed him were believers. Those people who refused to accept him, no longer believed, even though they accepted Moses' teachings. Those Christians were the "Believers" until Muhammad (S.A.W) came. After which any person claiming to believe and submitting to the will of God, Jehovah, Yahweh or Allah (S.W.T) must accept the Prophet Hood of Muhammad (S.A.W). Not doing so excommunicates them from belief.

822. **Q: Why do bad things happen?**

A: This existence that we as human beings cherish and cling to is nothing but a test to determine what should be our abode for eternity. Nothing good or bad in this world lasts forever, it is not permanent. The things we consider as "bad" may happen for several reasons:

As a punishment, such as the floods in the time of Noah. Or the destruction of Sodom and Gomorrah in the time of Lot.

Sometimes Allah (S.W.T) will afflict something upon us as a reminder, so that we may repent and reform ourselves.

Suffering can be a test of one's patience and steadfastness. Even the Prophets were made to suffer, such as Job. It is during these times that one can draw nearer to Allah (S.W.T).

Sometimes another person's suffering may be a test. To see how one reacts to the sick, needy or the infirm. One is tested in charity and faith.

823. **Q: How many Muslims are there in the world?**
A: There are over 1.5 billion Muslims in the world today. Around 2–3 million of them live in the UK. The most heavily populated countries, by number not percentage, are India and Indonesia

258

with around 175,000,000 (175 million) Muslims in each one.

824. **Q: Are all Arabs Muslim?**

A: About 92% of Arabs are Muslim. The other 8% is a mix of Jews, Christians, Atheists, Agnostics, Assyrians, Zoroastrians, etc. Although anyone who speaks Arabic uses the word "Allah" for God.

825. **Q: What is a Fatwa?**

A: It is a religious ruling to a question. It is based on Islamic law from the Quran, *Hadith and Sunnah.*

826. **Q: What is the difference between Hadith and Sunnah?**

A: *Hadith* are actual quotes of Muhammad (S.A.W). *Sunnah* is his deeds and actions or the deeds and actions performed by people in his presence of which he did not disapprove.

827. **Q: Why do women cover themselves?**

A: They do it in submission to Allah (S.W.T). He (Allah) asked them to cover their beauty and they do so. Most do so willingly and under Islamic law it is their own choice. Some cultures enforce it, and this is a contentious issue. Women that choose to wear the *Hijab* (Head covering) have been quoted as saying they find it empowering as they are no longer judged on their looks but on their aptitude. The concept of hijab is not unique to Islam. A Nuns' wimple and habit are the same as a hijab and kameez.

828. **Q: Is there anything about human rights in Islam?**

A: Freedom of conscience is laid down empathically in the Quran. "There is no compulsion in (accepting) the religion." The life, property and honour of all citizens of an Islamic state is considered sacred, whether the person is a Muslim or not.

829. **Q: James, I know you have been reading the Quran since your son got married to Islam so you must know it all.**

A: Nobody knows all about Monotheism except the author of the creation of the Universe – God (Allah).

830. **Q: What is Hadith?**

A: Hadith is an original text quote and unquote of Prophet Muhammad.

831. **Q: What is Sunnah?**

A: It is approved or witnessed actions and deeds of an individual. In Islam, it mostly refers to the Prophet's (Muhammad) deeds and actions.

832. **Q: Do Islamic people have a better chance to go to Heaven?**

A: God is not partial to anyone who obeys and follows God's commandments; they could enter Heaven.

833. **Q: What about unbelievers?**

A: Yes, if they repent now.

834. **Q: What about me?**

A: You are the only illegal occupant of earth who God has guaranteed you Hell.

835. **Q: Is it true that all Arabs are Muslims?**

A: No. There are approximately 1.6 million Muslims of which only 20% are Arabs.

836. **Q: Do all Arabs belong to Islam?**

A: No. About 92% of Arabs are Muslims, 8% non-Muslims belonging to Christianity, Agnostic, Atheists, Jews, Assyrians.

837.   **Q: Is it true that every Muslim must learn the Arabic language?**

A: Yes, by all and other monotheists. Islam summarise Allah as All Knowing All Seeing.

838.   **Q: I get you, James. Why? No choice for Muslims?**

A: All Muslims must learn the Arab language so that they can pray at least the five times in Arabic. It is a requirement.

839.   **Q: Do Islam celebrate Prophet Muhammad's birthday?**

A: No.

840.   **Q: What do the Islam think of Christians unity in God?**

A: Some Christians accept and believe in the Trinity, i.e. God the father, the son and Holy Spirit.

841.   **Q: What about the Islam?**

A: The Islam will like to say they believe in oneness of God, because God is the only one. Islam believe God is one in one. His sovereignty belongs to him alone.

842. **Q: What is the meaning of the five pillars of Islam that Islamic teaches?**

A: 1. To confirm that there is no other God worthy of worshipping and that Prophet Muhammad was God's messenger (declaration of faith); 2. Pray five times a day facing Makkah (prayer); 3. Donate a portion of your wealth to charity; 4. Sacrifice by going without food, drink, sex from dawn until sunset during Ramadan (fasting); 5. Perform the Haji at least once in your lifetime in Makkah (pilgrimage).

843. **Q: Don't you think Islam is asking too much of their followers?**

A: What are you not happy about, Satan? The content of the Holy book, the Quran, comes from Allah.

844. **Q: During Ramadan, why is there no sex or food or drink from 6a.m. to 6p.m., especially if the man has six wives?**

A: These are only for 40 days out of 365/366 days in a year. It helps them to get closer to God.

845. **Q: Who can question God of what he does?**

A: You are thinking of how you were thrown out of Heaven. Nobody dares question what the creator of the universe and what is in them. Not even his beloved son Jesus or Moses, Abraham, Jacob or Muhammad would have done so.

846. **Q: You said the Islam pray five times a day, is this compulsory, no excuses?**

A: It allows the Muslims to reflect, meditate and focus only on God and the true realities of life, the opportunities to worship, praise and glorify your creator is not much to ask for. I believe it is a recommendation, although Allah would have liked human to pray 50 times. Thanks to prophet Moses who it was believed begged God to reduced it to five days.

847. **Q: It is a lot – no choice for humans. You are obsessed with God. Why do the Islam perform rituals of washing etc. ablution before praying?**

A: There are rules for every successful action according to the faith. Prayers have spiritual and physical dimensions. Islam believe the ablution before prayers removes all impurities and it is necessary to be clean to present your praise, glorify and supplication to God.

848. **Q: In your previous answer to my question you said Islam must face Ka'ba in Makkah? Why?**

A: The first worshipping house was built by Adam in Ka'ba and rebuilt by Abraham and his son Ishmael. Islam believe therefore God has chosen Ka'ba as a starting point of *Unity* for all believers of God.

849. **Q: Do Muslims worship Muhammad?**

A: No. The Quran has emphasised many times that Prophet Muhammad was only one of God's true messengers. He was highly respected by all

265

mankind just as other prophets. He was the last prophet of Allah

850. **Q: But Christians worship Jesus Christ.**

A: No, Jesus could be a mediator/intermediary between man and God. But Christians do not worship Jesus. You can ask Jesus or any good prophet to pray to God for you.

851. **Q: Be honest, if Christians don't worship Christ why are the members called Christians after Christ?**

A: Satan you are talking nonsense again.

852. **Q: No. Muslims agree with me.**

A: It is no crime in religion/faith to express one's opinion. Do Buddhists worship Buddha, or Zoroastrians worship Zoroaster or Baha'u'llah? You, Satan, are full of...evil.

853. **Q: "Don't dream of any bad language unless you want to become my disciple," Satan said.**

A: Satan, go to hell where you belong, I am going to have a cup of tea.

854. **Q: "And don't forget to confess your thought of sin," said Satan**

A: The greater sin is the one who tempts people to sin live evilly, Satan. Just as you made Adam and Eve to sin.

855. **Q: On that note. What do the Islam regard as the greatest sin?**

A: To worship anybody or thing alongside God because you cannot serve two masters.

856. **Q: How many prophets are there up to Muhammad?**

A: There have been 124,000 prophets.

857. **Q: Name some of those prophets mentioned in the Quran.**

A: The Arch Angel gave the Quran 25 strong prophets, namely: Adam, Enoch, Noah, Abraham, Lot, King David, King Solomon, Jonah, Zachariah, John the Baptist, Jesus and Muhammad.

858. **Q: Does it mean the others were fake prophets?**

A: (Took a deep breath to calm down from Satan's nonsense) The Bible and Islam respect all the prophets including Jeremiah, Elijah, Elisha and Daniel.

859. **Q: How much do you respect Mary because she was the only woman revealed explicitly in the Quran?**

A: Good, Satan, you know your history.

860. **Q: (A gleam on his face)**

A: Muslims greatly respect Jesus' mother Mary as one of the greatest of all women. To confirm this there is one chapter (Surah 19), which the Arch Angel named after Mary.

861. **Q: What about Jesus?**

A: Muslims deeply respect Jesus as much as Muhammad. Both are regarded as amongst the greatest human beings/prophets of God.

862. **Q: Christians say Moses was a prophet of the Jews but Muslims say Moses was Muslim.**

A: Moses, like all the prophets up to Muhammad, were a prophet of God for all of mankind on earth. What Moses instructed the Israelites was to pray, fast and love – all are followed by all the prophets up to Muhammad.

863. **Q: So, what is special about the Quran and Muhammad?**

A: Islam believe Muhammad was the last prophet for all mankind, hence the Quran is for all faiths, including Christians, Jews, Hindus, Buddhists, Zoroastrians, Baha'l, etc.

864. **Q: What about other prophets?**

A: Theology tells us that most prophets were chosen for tribes, nations who God did not reveal important messages for all mankind.

865. **Q: Who will the Islam regard as prophets for mankind?**

A: I would think those 25 prophets' names in the Quran.

866. **Q: James, do not beat about the bush. Answer my question.**

A: (In my mind, I wouldn't let him annoy me) I would say those that God reveals the content of the Holy book to, i.e. a few prophets for Torah, David for the Psalms, the Old Testament revelations to Isaiah, Jeremiah, Daniel, etc. Jesus Christ (New Testament) and the enforcement of the Old Testament and Muhammad for the Quran.

867. **Q: Where do the Islam stand on Salvation?**

A: Anyone who believes in God alone as creator, forgives, prays for others, does good without expecting anything back, then through God's mercy, forgiveness, love and blessing that individual will be assured of salvation on Judgement day.

868. **Q: Do Islam accept other faiths?**

A: Islam says everybody has to accept Prophet Muhammad's teaching. Islam respect all religion.

869. **Q: What happens if one doesn't accept Muhammad?**

A: I am afraid Islam answer to this is that by not accepting Prophet Muhammad this would lead to excommunicating those people from being a true believer in God.

870. **Q: What was the estimated number of Muslims in the world in 2010?**

A: Approximately 1.7 billion Muslims.

871. **Q: Which country do you find the largest population of Muslims?**

A: India, Indonesia.

872. **Q: How many Muslims are there in each of these countries: UK, India, Indonesia?**

A: 2.3 million in the UK, 175 million in India ad 175 million in Indonesia.

873. **Q: Who do the Muslims pledge their allegiance to?**

A: Without a shadow of a doubt, Muslims pledge of allegiance is only to God, the creator, the overseer, the geometrician and sovereign God.

874. **Q: What proof is there of the Muslims' allegiance to God?**

A: Muslims must pledge daily and to recite it in groups verbally, non-verbally or privately or in silence.

875. **Q: What do Muslims say in their pledge?**

A: I bear witness that there is no one worthy of worship except Allah…and I bear witness that Prophet Muhammad is the Messenger of God.

876. **Q: Where do the Muslims stand with invading other countries?**

A: Islam regard invading and killing people is one of the greatest crimes against God.

877. **Q: Where do Islam stand with Human Rights?**

A: This is answered in the Quran 2:256, "There shall be no compulsion in what religion one chooses."

Also, in Quran 49:13 state, "O mankind, indeed God has created you, male and female, and made you people and tribes that you may know one another. Indeed, the most noble of you in the sight of God is the most righteous of you. Indeed, God is Knowing and Acquainted."

878. **Q: Why is it that Muslims don't show kindness?**

A: Satan, you are wrong; there are verses in the Quran to support that Muslims are kind:

"...be kind as Allah has been kind to you..." (Quran 28:77)

"Be kind to your parents and relatives and the orphans, and those in need, and speak nicely to people." (Quran 2:83)

879. **Q: I have met a lot of young Muslims who are not polite to people.**

A: In all faiths, young or old, people may behave in impolite ways, but the Quran teaches the Islam to be polite.

880. **Q: I guess you can quote from the Quran**

A: To convince you and your evil followers, "Hence, the modest in your behaviour and lower your voice: for behold, the ugliest of all voices is the harshest voice of a donkey." (Quran 31:19)

881. **Q: Do Islam people do not show fairness and justice?**

A: Satan, you may be talking to people that have left Islam and joined you, but I can unequivocally assure you that the decent people of Muslims are fair and always implement justice.

882. **Q: James have you read the Quran and spoken to any of the Iman?**

A: Of course, but where do you think I got all the information from?

"Allah commands Justice and Fairness." (Quran 16:90)

"...Let not the hatred of others make you do wrong and depart from Justice. Be just, that is next to piety." (Quran 5:8)

Also, "...stand out firmly for justice, as witnesses for Allah..." (Quran 4:135)

883. **Q: What about generosity to other people who are not Muslims?**

A: "Those who spend their money for the sake of Allah night and day both privately and publicly, will get their reward from their Lord. They shall have no cause to fear nor shall they grieve." (Quran 2:274)

884. **Q: Islam taught people not to forgive, that they should practice Mosaic Law "Eye for an eye" and "tooth for a tooth".**

A: On the question of forgiveness, it is clear in the Quran, for example, "The good deed and evil deed are not alike. Repel the evil deed with one that is better, then lo! The person who was your enemy may become like a close friend." (Quran 41:34)

In fact, "Practice forgiveness, command decency and avoid ignorant people." (Quran 7:199)

885. **Q: How many prayers in Islamist?**

A: Five prayers of Islam are related to the five pillars of fate. These also relate to the posture which all have meanings. The five times is the minimum and must be done according to the time of day, hence the changes.

886. **Q: How many times do Islam pray to Allah?**

A: Islam can pray to Allah as many times as an individual wants to put their supplication in addition to the minimum. The parlance is the same.

887. **Q: What is the purpose of the prayers?**

A: The prayers unite the mind, soul and body in worshipping God. The prayers for the five sets are the same. So, in effect, all Islam in Britain may be praying at the same time.

888. **Q: What language are prayers recited in?**

A: The set prayers are recited in Arabic, which may make it difficult for non-Islam to be part of the congregation. Non-Muslims who convert to Islam must learn the prayers in Arabic.

889. **Q: How many postures are there during prayers?**

A: There are about ten postures. During prayer, they are strictly forbidden to look round, must be in a state of deep concentration to be in the presence of Allah/God.

890. **Q: What is the 1st prayer to start after ablution?**

A: First *Takbir (Allahu Akbar)*: Takbir is entering the state of prayer by glorifying God. Muslims face towards Makkah, standing with their hands raised to the level of their ears or shoulders and make the intention to pray.

To begin the act of prayer, they say Allahu Akbar, meaning God is great.

891. **Q: What is the 2nd stage in prayers**

A: Second *Qiyama*: Muslims place their right hand over their left on their chest or navel while in the standing position (this may vary according to the subdivision followed).

A short supplication glorifying God and seeking His protection is read. This is then followed by Surah Al Fatima which is the first chapter in the Quran. Verses from any other chapters are then recited.

892. **Q: Describe the 3 rd posture and its meaning.**

A: Roku which means bowing. They say sub Hana Rib al Anthem three times. It means "Glory be to God, the Greatest."

To move from one posture to another you say, "God listen to the one who praises."

893. **Q: Describe the 4th posture.**

A: Moving into an upright position you recite Sa Me Aah Allahu Lamen Hamedah, "God listens to the one who praises him."

While in a standing position recite, "To God belongs all praise," then recite, "God is Great."

The hands must be loosely at the sides and legs together.

Each movement is always preceded by the phrase "God is Great", which tells the congregation that the leader is about to change posture.

894. **Q: Describe the 5th posture.**

A: *Sujud (Allahu Akbar)*: Sujud means to prostrate.

Then recite "Sub-Hana Rabi al Aalah". It means "Glory be to God, the Highest," which must be repeated three times.

N.B. In this position only palms, knees, toes, forehead and nose are the only parts of the body that may touch the ground.

Prophet Muhammad said, "The worst thief is the one who abstains or steals from his prayer."

His companions ask, "O Messenger of Allah, how does he steal from his prayer?" He replied, "He does not perfect its Tuku and sujud."

895. **Q: Describe the 6 th posture.**

A: Briefly sitting (Allahu Akbar): "God is Great" is recited while moving into a sitting position. Muslims pause here for a few seconds, either staying silent or reciting a shorter prayer. "God is Great" is recited once more as the "sujud" position is taken again (see "3" above). At this position the prophet recommends that each movement must last at least the time that it takes for the bones to settle. He compares some people's ruku and sujud to the way that a crow pecks on the ground, because of the speed at which they perform it (ibn Khuzaymah).

896. **Q: Describe the 7 th posture.**

A: *Sujud (*Allahu *Akbar)* same as the first one.

(Sub hana Rabi Al Aalah) "raka'ah" or unit is complete after reciting "Glory be to God, the Highest." Each salah has its own number of units though – Fajr has two. To continue the prayer from the sujud position, Muslims say, "God is Great" and then stand up to repeat everything from Surah Al Fatiha, until they reach this sujud again.

897. **Q: Describe the 8** **th** **posture.**

A: *Tashahhud (Allahu Akbar)*: After saying God is Great, Muslims return to the sitting position. They recite a set number of short prayers in Arabic, praising God and sending peace on the prophet. They repeat the declaration of faith, raising of their right hand to act as a witness.

They then ask God to bestow blessing and peace upon Prophet Abraham and his family and ask for the same for Prophet Muhammad. Finally, the Muslims ask for forgiveness and mercy, and ask God to bless them and their children until the Day of Judgement.

898. **Q: Describe the 9 th posture.**

A: *As Salamo Ala Ikom Wa Rah Mati Allah* (Peace to the right): To the end of the prayer Muslims first turn their face to the right saying, "Peace be upon you, and the mercy and blessings of Allah." This is said to the angels; which Muslims believe accompany each human being to record their actions.

899. **Q: Describe the 10 th posture.**

A: As Salamo Ala Ikom Wa Rah Mati Allah (Peace to the left). "Peace be upon you, and the mercy and blessings of Allah" is repeated turning to the left side now.

900. **Q: What is syncretism?**

A: This is when one believes that there is truth in all religions, that everybody is worshipping God in his own way and that all religions ultimately lead to the same God. No matter how popular this "faith", is becoming today, and no matter who believes it, it is a doctrine of demons. (John 14:6) Each faith must sort their own internal division. Accept the faith.

901. **Q: How many sects are there of Islam?**

A: 150 sects.

902. **Q: Is Allah the same as God?**

A: Yes – Colossians 1:3 "God and the Father of our Lord Jesus Christ."

903. **Q: What are the main faith groups of Muslims?**

A: Sunnism, Sufism, Shi'itism, Wahhabism, Ahmadiyya and Bahai.

904. **Q: What is love?**

A: This can be found in 1 John 4:17–18: "There is no fear in love, but *perfect love* casts out fear...our love made perfect."

905. **Q: How long has the Quran been in existence?**

A: According to Surah 6:92, 3:7, 43:3–4 stated that the content of the Quran existed before the creation of the world. Surah 53:4 says the Quran is a Divine Revelation sent down.

906. **Q: The Quran was sent down by who?**

A: Surah 3:3, 4:105, 4:113, 31:21, 42:17, 76:23 – show that the book was sent down by Allah.

907. **Q: Can one question the Quran?**

A: According to Ta'abbudi – the Quran must be accepted without questions or without criticism.

908. **Q: Who gave the book to Muhammad?**

A: According to Surah 26:192–194, 16:102 says Muhammad received the Quran from "The Holy Spirit".

909. **Q: What is between Islam (causing division)?**

A: Quarrelling, fighting, undermining and killing in his name. Surah 5:36 – All those who opposed Muhammad's message be killed or nailed on a tree or cut their hands and legs off or get thrown out of the city. (Surah 5:36)

In Surah 47:4 – Muslims told to smite the neck of all those who do not accept his teaching or arrested and to pay a ransom. (Surah 2:190–121, 9:19–22, 29, 41)

Surah 47:4 – non-believers smite at their neck and until many unbelievers were killed.

Anyone who leaves Islam should be slain. (Surah 4:89)

910. **Q: Do Christians love Islam?**

A: Christians love everybody and even their Muslim enemies. (Surah 5:82–85)

911. **Q: Are there evil spirits?**

A: We wrestle against flesh and blood but against the rulers of darkness of the world, against principalities, against spiritual wickedness in high places and therefore weapons of our warfare are not carnal (physical arm, cutlasses, swords, guns, knives, matches, petrol, bow and arrows), but mighty through God to the pulling down of a stronghold. (2 Corinthians 10:4; Ephesians 6:12)

912. **Q: Why do Muslims say, "God's curse be on them" which sometimes refer to Christians?**

A: Because Christians insist Jesus is the son of God. The Quran questions how God can have a son when he has no consort. (Surah 6:10)

913. **Q: Did or has God got a wife?**

A: No. Around the fifth and seventh centuries it was believed that God the Creator had a wife called Venus or Al Zahrah who was regarded as the "Queen of Heaven" who was Mary that Jesus was their son by proclamation. That was why they said that Mary was worshipped as the Queen (Marianist).

914. **Q: Do the Islam believe in the Trinity?**

A: No – Christians believe God the Father, the son and Holy Spirit but Islam (Surah 5:119) disbelieve. It can be argued that if Mary was the Queen of Heaven, then why did the trinity say God the Father, the son and Holy Spirit.

915. **Q: What did the Quran say about Jesus' birth?**

A: The Quran has no problem with the divinity of Jesus/Mary. The Bible says, "God is a spirit". They agree but insist that Jesus was the spirit of God that came into Mary his mother. (Surah 21:91)

916. **Q: Why did the prophesy in the Old Testament say a prophet would be born and named Immanuel?**

A: Immanuel means "God is with us".

The Bible refers to Jesus as the Word of God. (John 1:1, 14) In the Quran the angels said, "O Mary, God giveth thee glad tidings of a Word from Him. His name will be Christ Jesus the son of Mary."

917. **Q: Why is the Trinity proclaimed to be one with 1 + 1 + 1 = 3?**

A: Because God the Father, the son and Holy Spirit are one spiritually. One can say the Trinity is a spirit, soul and body; hence God can review himself in this Trinity.

918. **Q: What did the Angel say to Mary?**

A: In Luke 1:35 God sent the Angel Gabriel to announce to Mary, "The Holy Ghost shall come upon thee and the power of the Highest shall overshadow thee; therefore also the Holy One which shall be born of thee shall be called the Son of God."

Comment: If one believes in Hindus Lord Krishna and believes in reincarnation then both Jesus and Krishna are attributes of God.

919. **Q: How did St. Paul add to the confusion of false prophet?**

A: Before Muhammad St. Paul warned, "But though we as an angel from Heaven preach any other gospel unto you than that which we have preached unto you let him be accursed." (Galatians 1:8)

"Thou art my beloved son; in thee I am well pleased." (Luke 3:22)

"Let God be true, but every man a liar." (Romans 3:4)

920. **Q: Can God's word be corrupted?**

A: Surah 6:34 and 10:64 state that corruption at the word of God is utterly impossible. God is in control of His word.

921. **Q: How many translations are there of the Quran?**

A: There are about 50 different translations of the Quran. I have read a few and the more I read different translations the more confused and contradictory it becomes.

922. **Q: How do Muslims perceive Adam and Jesus?**

A: Surah 3:59 said that Jesus was created a being just as Adam was and is no more a son of God than Adam was. Hence Muslims will not bow down to Jesus.

923. **Q: Did God ask angels to worship Adam?**

A: To bow to Adam NOT worship. There are at least seven places in the Quran that show this. (Surah 18:50, 7:11, 15:29–35, 17:61–62, 18:50, 20:115, 38:174)

924. **Q: Was Jesus created by God?**

A: God had Jesus before the creation of the Universe. Islam argued the relationship of Adam and Jesus. (Surah 3:59)

925. **Q: What did God say about Jesus in the Quran?**

A: The Surah 21:91 says Jesus was/is our spirit.

926. **Q: Is Christian Heaven the same as Islamist Heaven?**

A: Since there is only one God as Prophet Muhammad said that both Christians and Islam have one thing in common, i.e. worship the same God.

This proves there must be one Paradise God where God, prophets, saint, men of God and Angels live.

Islam feels that there are seven Heavens and it depends on the outcome of Judgement on everyone. One quality of sin will decide which Heaven they go to.

927. **Q: Will there be marriage and sex in Heaven?**
A: According to Surah 56:10–38 the answer was yes. A portion in a different Quran described this. Surah 55:50–55 (Pure wives), Surah 3:15 (Al Hilali), Surah 37:48, 44:50–55 (A.J. Asberry).

One of the Hadith says, "The lowliest inhabitant of the Paradise will be he who has 8,000 servants, 72 wives," – page 204 at Mishkat al-Masabih sh-m Ashraf (1990).

Some Muslims believe Allah will give permission to have sexual intercourse (ibid p.1200).

928. **Q: How many wives did Muhammad have?**

A: This is conflicting information: 27, 29, 9, 11, 13. It confirmed that the prophet did not have any other wife until the first wife died.

929. **Q: Name some of the Prophet's wives.**

A: Aisha (Ayesha), Hafsa, Safia, Sawda, Un Salama, Zainab, Mariam, Umma, Habiba, Maymuna, Raihana, Juwayriya and Safiyya. And many more names from Ali-Dashi.

In Surah 33:50, the Prophet gave permission to have more wives.

930. **Q: How many children did the Prophet have?**

A: One girl, Fatima. He adopted a son Zaid, who had a girl Zainab. It is reported that the Prophet divorced the mother and he married Zaid.

931. **Q: Was there prostitution in Mecca during Hajj?**

A: Arguably yes. But this was discouraged and did not last for long. A few people gave me this information.

932. **Q: Did Allah gave permission for men to beat their wives?**

A: Yes. (Surah 4:34). Allah gave permission to beat wives if they misbehaved. This appears not to happen in this modern time due to the laws of the country whereby women are treated equal to some extent.

933. **Q: What about Christians men with wives?**

A: Ephesians 5:25–33; Colossians 3:19; 1 Corinthians 7:2–5: No punishment to wives.

934. **Q: Is there wine in Muslim Heaven?**

A: Yes. (Surah 47:15, 76:5, 21, 83:23–29) Rivers of wine. Muslims are not allowed to drink alcoholic wine.

935. **Q: How do Islam perceive the soul?**

A: Islam, Hindus, Sikhs, Buddhists believe that all souls were created before the flesh and body.

Comment: This brings to light reincarnation. When one dies the soul then comes back in a different form, e.g. African or European, man or woman, rich or poor.

I, the author, believe that God has created a specific number of souls who keep coming back. It means during Judgement day on souls could have come back or reincarnated so many times. For example, 20 or 40 times.

So, on Judgement day there may be one soul representing about 40 humans.

936. **Q: What is Islam?**

A: It is a faith in one Allah, it is a religion, morally, socially, politically, economically, ideologically.

937. **Q: Do Muslims believe Jesus will come back to Judge?**

A: A booklet by www.fisabililah.org *The Journey: A Brief Guide* (page 8), stated that Jesus will return near the end of time.

But Muslims believe God will come to Judge. Nobody knows who the judge on judgement day will be.

938. **Q: What do Islam think of Jesus?**

A: They do not believe in the Trinity, do not believe Jesus died – they think Jesus was raised to Heaven. They do not believe the cross, they do not believe Jesus was the son of God, which is regarded in the Arab world as blasphemy.

939. **Q: How many wives does Islam allow men?**

A: Although polygamy is practiced, in recent years it was recommended that men must not have not more than four and to avoid abandoning the women.

940. **Q: What is the Islamic legal code?**

A: It is known as Shari ah.

941. **Q: Do Islam aim for perfection?**

A: No, because no human is infallible except God's (Allah) messengers, like Jesus, Abraham or Muhammad.

942. **Q: Name Islamic five Pillars.**

A: 1. Shahadah: Declaration of faith is that there is no God but Allah. This is clear that no other god but Allah. Also, Islam can only learn what Allah dictates to Prophet Abraham; 2. Salah: Allah is a Creator and supreme power; 3. Sawm; 4. Zakah; 5. Hajt.

943. **Name the Prayers (daily)**

A: Morning twilight before sunrise (Fajr); b. Zuhr (noon); c. Maghrib (after sunset); d. Isha.

The aim of these prayers serves the Islam as an ongoing reminder of our purpose in life and prevents us from straying too far off the path.

944. **Q: Who do the Quran say started the Islam?**

A: The Muslims claim that Adam, Abraham and all the prophets up to the death of Jesus (including Jesus) were Islam. In effect Islam existed before Prophet Muhammed received the revelation for the whole world

945. **Q: Jesus is reported to have come came as a spirit of God for all mankind but what were the Romans 8:9 discrimination by Paul?**

A: "If any man has not the spirit of Christ, he is none of his – even if he has well-known religion". Jesus is reported to have said that he came to divide but not to unite. This prophesy was evidence in current years.

946. **Q: Can anyone have the spirit of Christ even if he is not a Christian?**

A: If the person accepts Christ, yes – like Muslims they accept Christ, say 95% of the people I talk to.

947. Q: John 1:12 state that, "But as many as received him, to them gave power?"

A: The power is a privilege, right, authority and with these powers one becomes the sons of God (also 2 Corinthians 1:22).

948. Q: What does Psalm 32:1 mean by atonement (covering)?

A: "Blessed is he whose transgression is forgiven whose sin is covered". This is covered by God or Jesus.

949. Q: In Philippians 3:3–10 Apostle Paul gave a long speech/letter, thus he discriminated against some Christians who are not 100% Christians. Did any of the prophet followers behave in that way?

A: Paul went from 100% against Christians to 100% supporter of Christ. He was a committed Christian. None of prophet's close friends deserted him.

950. Q: If the Quran accepted the Old Testament, e.g. Genesis, why was there contradiction on how long it took for the world to be created?

A: One needs to be careful of the wording. Surah 54:50 said the world was created in seconds; Surah 4:19 said two days; verse 10, four days; verse 12 says seven Heavens; Surah 7:54 says six days – Surah 10:3 and 32:4. The old testament of the Bible stated that God created the world in six days.

951. **Q: The Quran says a lot of good things about Jesus and then contradicts each other. Name some examples?**

A: Islam believe in divinity, that it may be Jesus who might come back to judge all of mankind.

952. **Q: Where in the Bible does it talk about Jesus being the son of God? Do Muslims believe in that?**

A: Proverbs 30:4 and 2 Peter 1:16–19. No Islam do not believe he was the son of God. In fact, most of the monotheists believe that we are all children of Allah.

953. **Q: What do you think supports that God of the Christians is the same as Allah or Muslims?**

A: The Quran in Surah 9:30 has vigorously objected the Christians saying Jesus Christ is the son of God. It went further to say God's curse be on them and, in fact, it said that the Christians were deluded away from the truth. (Surah 9:30).

954. **Q: What did the Bible and the Quran say God is?**

Both said God is a spirit, all knowing, all seeing and is the alpha and Omega

955. **Q: What did the Quran say Jesus on earth was?**

A: The Quran says Jesus is the spirit of God that came into Mary. (Surah 21:91)

956. **Q: How does one know who is "The Word"?**

A: In John 1:1, 14 it supports that Jesus was the word. "…and the word was made flesh and dwelt among us."

In Surah 3:45 the Quran said the angels said to Mary, "O Mary! God giveth thee glad tidings of a word from Him. His name will be Christ Jesus the son of Mary."

957. **Q: What does the Gospel mean?**

A: The Christians interpretation of the Gospel means Good News.

958. **Q: The Bible says a thousand years is a day for God (figuratively speaking). What about the Quran?**

A: Surah 32:5 says 1000 years is a day for God; Surah 70:4 says 50 years is a day for Allah.

959. **Q: When Christians say, "By the Grace of God" what are they referring to?**

A: God has favoured an individual that was not expected.

960. **Q: What does ablution mean in the Quran?**

A: The washing of face, hands and rubbing of the head before Muslims start praying. (Surah 5:7 and 4:43) – washing away sin before praying.

961. **Q: What do the Christians say about clean hands?**

A: The Christians mean clean spirit not physically. Psalm 24:3–4, Jeremiah 2:22, Isaiah 59:3–8 or 1 John 1:7 (blood of Christ cleanses us from all sin).

962. **Q: How many times was Hell and Paradise mentioned in the Quran?**

A: Hell was 83, Paradise four. The Quran refers to paradise as garden instead of paradise.

963. **Q: Is God in Heaven?**

A: In Muslim's Heaven God will not be there, there will be no worship as they have done enough on earth.

964. **Q: Will man see God?**

A: Blessed are the pure in heart, for they shall see God. (Matthew 5:8) Also John 4:22, John 14:1–6.

965. **Q: Who is in Heaven?**

A: For Christians' Heaven, God and Jesus will be there. (1 John 3:2; Revelation 22:3–4) From the Muslim perspective, God and all the angels and some of the prophets' spirits will be there.

966. **Q: Where in the Bible can we find drunkenness?**

A: Galatians 5:19–21; Ephesians 5:5–7.

967. **Q: Is there alcohol in Christians Heaven?**

A: No – nor meat nor drink but righteousness, peace and joy in the Holy Ghost. (Romans 14:17; Matthew 26:26–29; 1 Timothy 5:23)

In Christian Heaven, there is water of life, not rivers of wine. (Revelation 21:6–8, 22:1–2)

968. **Q: What has God prepared for Christian Heaven?**

A: Jesus' Heaven (1 Corinthians 2:9); Matthew 22:30; John 12:49–50).

969. **Q: What is the Christian marriage super?**

A: This can be found in Revelation 19:7–9. (Ephesians 5:25–32)

970. **Q: Where do we find in the Quran about marriage?**

A: Surah 44:54, 52:20, Surah 56:20 A.J. Asberry – Quran; for Christian Heaven Matthew 22:29–30; Mark 12:24–25.

971. **Q: What do Muslims regard as life?**

A: Life is of "The Three W's" – wine, women and war.

972. **Q: Can God or Allah decide to intentionally mislead a person from the way of salvation if he chooses to?**

A: Allah is the same as a Christian God; he created humans and can do whatever he chooses to.

The Quran always mentions possibly every IV pages that Allah is all knowing, all merciful, all forgiving, all wise and has promised humans (through Prophet Muhammad and Jesus) that whosoever abides by the Ten Commandments will have a ticket to Heaven.

In the Bible John 8:12 Jesus said, "…I am the light of the world, he that followed me shall not walk in darkness but shall have the light of life." Also 1 Timothy 2:4; 2 Peter 3:9): "Who will have all men to be saved, and to come into the knowledge of the truth." In Matthew 25:41 Jesus said Hell was created for Satan and his angels.

The Quran beyond doubt stated Allah can decide to mislead a person from the way of

Salvation if he chooses to. (Surah 16:93, 13:27, 25:9)

But Surah 74:31 says that Allah leads astray whom He will and guides him whom Allah He will.

In Surah 14:4 we read, "Allah misleads whom he will and guides whom He will."

Now when we look at Surah 4:88 – it warns that nobody should lead a person who has been led astray by Allah to the way of salvation.

In Surah 7:179: "Many are the Jinn's and men we have made for Hell."

All the above quotations come from Dr. M.T. Al-Hilali and Dr Muhsin Khan's translation.

If God/Allah decides to lead anybody to Hell then I expect readers to ask more questions of the Muslims, especially consider what the Quran describes Allah as All-mighty, the All-wise, All merciful.

God even accepted saint Paul who murdered hundreds of Christians to lead Christians.

I reserve my judgement and leave God to decide which is in line of Prophet Muhammad.

973. **Q: What is one reason Jesus came to earth?**

A: To fulfil the Ten Commandments, "That all things which are written may be fulfilled." (Luke 21:22)

974. **Q: As the Jews rejected Jesus, what was their reward?**

A: Remember Psalm 91 – The righteous will see the rewards of wickedness. In Luke 21:24 Jesus said, "...and Jerusalem shall be trodden down at the Gentiles, until the times of the Gentiles (non-Jews) be fulfilled."

975. **Q: What are the Crusades?**

A: The Crusades in history were a political war involving the king's emperors. The Apostle Papacy initially wanted to join due to the stability of Jerusalem.

976. **Q: Was Jesus's prophesies fulfilled?**

A: Yes. In 70AD General Titus destroyed the Jews' Temple and drove the Jews away.

638AD Muslims took over Jerusalem and were reported to have killed over 80,000 Jews. They built a mosque near where King Solomon was.

977. **Q: Name the main duties of all Muslims.**

A: There are five practical/vital duties expected from Muslims or Islam: 1. Fasting (sawn), a fast for daylight hours during the ninth lunar month of Ramadan; 2. Hajj – pilgrimage to Mecca. It is recommended for every Muslim to make this journey once in their lifetime; 3. Zakat – it is compulsory to make a contribution towards welfare, to support the poor; 4. Salat – there must be five daily prayers; 5. Shahada – All Muslims to emphasise their faith, that Allah is the only God and that Muhammad is Allah's messenger.

978. **Q: According to Surah 9:19 what are the three things that attract rewards for Muslims?**

A: These are Jihad, belief in Allah and belief in Last Day of Judgement.

979. **Q: What are the main faiths as seen by the Muslims?**

A:

- Belief in angels (good and bad)
- Belief in the Holy books – Quran, Torah, Psalms and Gospel. Except for the Quran, the

rest are an acknowledgement of corrupted Holy books.

- Belief in the prophets, which include Jesus, Muhammad and all the prophets in the Old Testament.

980. **Q: Did Prophet Muhammad suffer?**

A: Yes. He suffered psychologically, physically and emotionally. Psychologically because his first wife died.

All her male children died, and he was only left with one female daughter Fatima. Physically he was beaten, humiliated and called all kinds of nasty names, such as deluded and hallucination. Enemies tried to kill him and he and Abu Bakr ran and hid in a cave where God protected them with a spider web. Their friends had to supply them with food and water.

981. **Q: How did the prophet and his companion survive this ordeal they overcome this?**

A: God, through the angel, helped them to escape to a foreign country Medina.

982. **Q: Why didn't Prophet Muhammad's family protect him?**

A: I am told that his own family (after his wife died) plotted to kill him as he was rich – he inherited from his wife.

983. **Why didn't the Angel punish his enemies if he was carrying out God's mission?**

A: I was told that the Angel asked the Prophet if he wanted God to punish his enemies, but he said no.

984. **Q: What happened to Muhammad in the cave?**

A: I understand he was beaten by a scorpion.

985. **Q: Why were people jealous of him?**

A: Because not everybody wanted to adopt the content of the Quran. Muslims did not want any more hardship (the Quran being a way of life).

986. **Q: Who led the revolt against Muhammad?**

A: Abu Lahab from his own tribe was his worst enemy.

987. **Q: What is the name of his tribe?**

A: Qurash.

988. **Q: Why are there no pictures of Muhammad?**

A: As a means of respect so that he is not misrepresented.

989. **Q: Why do some Muslim men have long beards?**

A: It was assumed that prophets had beards.

990. **Q: Do Muslims believe in reincarnation (life after death)?**

A: Yes.

991. **Q: How do we know Prophet Muhammad was the last prophet of God?**

A: He did not leave any male child to become a prophet. In the Britannica Encyclopaedia Jesus was supposed to have said, "There is only one prophet to come after me who will show you the right path."

992. **Q: Give about 20 Arab traditions and proverbs?**

A: He is not good who abandons the world for the sake of life after death; similarly, there is not good in him who rejects the hereafter for the sake of this worldly life. But there is good in him who accepts both. (Islamic Tradition)

The believer says little but performs much, whereas the hypocrite says much but performs little. (Al-Awza)

Listen and keep silent, behold and wonder. (al-Tawhidi)

It is written in ancient scripture that divine mercy is only given to those who are merciful to Allah's creation. (Tawhidi)

Allah (S.W.T) did not create a disease without creating a cure for it.

Patience is half of faith and certitude is complete faith.

Whoever does not command justice and condemn injustice, Allah (S.W.T) alone destroys him.

In Islam Allah (S.W.T) curses both giver and receiver of bribes or gifts to tax-collectors.

Be kind to your neighbour.

You shall not be a believer, until you love your fellow believer as yourself.

If a young man honours an older person because of his age, Allah (S.W.T) will choose someone to honour him in his old age. (Prophet Muhammad (S.A.W))

Muhammad (S.A.W) said: "Do not be angry because anger leads to violent quarrels and fighting."

Whosoever fasts in the month of Ramadan with strong faith and good conscience, will have all his previous sins forgiven by Allah (S.W.T).

It is Allah's (S.W.T) commandment that every Muslim bathes (washes the whole body) at least once a week; and that they wash the head and other parts of the body.

A learned man among ignorant people is like a living person who walks over the backs of dead people. (Prophet Muhammad (S.A.W))

There is no greater calamity than ignorance. (Arab Proverb)

Ignorance is the death of living beings. (Al-Tha'alibi al-Tambil)

Lying is a sickness and truth is a cure. (Al-Maydani Amthali)

A man must not disfigure their wives and is not to use obscene language against them.

You must always respect your elderly so that the same be done for you.

993. **Q: What is the significance of Islam's last prayer?**

A: The last prayer is the key to divine mercy. (Arab Proverb)

994. **Q: What does Islam say about meditation?**

A: An hour's contemplation is more meritorious than sixty years of worship. (Ali al-Mulaqi)

995. **Q: What are the three noble deeds?**

A: Remembrance of Allah (S.W.T) alone in all circumstances, fairness to mankind and beneficence to his brethren. (Ali al-Mulaqi)

996. **Q: What is Islam's view on suicide?**

A: Committing suicide in any form is forbidden and will be condemned to everlasting Hellfire.

997. **Q: What was Muhammad's view on hypocrites?**

A: Muhammad (S.A.W) is reported to have said: "The hypocrite is like a hesitant (confused) goat torn between two herds, sometimes he goes to one, and sometimes he goes to the other. He does not know which of the two to follow." (Translated by M. Hamidullah)

998. **Q: What happens in Ramadan?**

A: During the month of Ramadan, the gates of Paradise (blessings) are opened and the gates of Hellfire are shut down, and the devils are put in fetters.

999. **Q: Muhammad (S.A.W) said: "Allah (S.W.T) smiles at two persons; one of whom having killed the other, yet both entering paradise. How is that?"**

A: He was asked: "The one killed in the path of Allah (S.W.T), so is a martyr, he entered paradise. Thereafter Allah (S.W.T) accepted the repentance of the other and guided him to Islam where, after he joined the struggle and was also killed in the way of Allah (S.W.T) and fell as a martyr."

1000. Q: Muhammad's (S.A.W) view of women was?

A: "You feed her when you eat, you clothe her as you clothe yourself, do not smite her on her face, do not insult her and do not leave her alone, except at home."

1001. Q: Muhammad (S.A.W) addressed the pilgrims during his farewell pilgrimage, what did he say?

A: "O Mankind you have rights over your wives, just as they have rights over you. You have the right to expect that they will never let anyone else lie on your marital bed in your absence, and that she or they will not behave in an unlawful manner. If they do so the Allah (S.W.T) gives you the right to separate them from your bed, and the right to inflict physical punishment to discipline them. If they cease to misbehave then you must always supply them their daily food, and clothing. Treat your women well. You have accepted them as your wives and as a trust from Allah. Allah alone made it legitimate for you, the enjoyment of their persons, by the word of Allah."

1002. **Q: In 19:29–33 what did God give to Prophet Muhammad?**

A: So, she pointed to him, "They said how can we speak to a baby in the cradle?" I am the slave of Allah. He gave me the book and made me a Prophet. And he blessed wherever I am and charged me with prayers and charity so long as I live.

"Benevolent to my mother. He has not made me a miserable tyrant.

Peace unto me the day I was born, the day I die and the day I am resurrected."

1003. **Q: According to Quran 9:40 what did Prophet Muhammad say to his companion in the cave?**

A: When those who deny drove him out, one of the two was he in the cave when he told his companion, "Do not grieve, for Allah is with us so Allah sent down his peace upon him and supported him by soldiers you could not see and let the word of the deniers go under, and the word of Allah is the highest."

Allah is of the highest wisdom of invincible Will.

1004. **Q: How did God save Muhammad in the cave?**

A: Muhammad and Abu Baker were hiding in a cave and as the people were looking to kill them, it was reported that miraculously, the entrance of the cave was covered with the tree of a spider web. Then they found a wild dove that had built its nest in the tree.

1005. **Q: If Allah created everything, then who created Allah?**

A: Say Allah is one, Allah the everlasting. He has not given birth, He was not born, and He has absolutely no peer. (Quran 112)

1006. **Q: What does Al Quran 5:49 say about sinners?**

A: And decided between them according to what Allah has shown you and do not follow their wishes. If they turn away, then know what Allah desires to Strike them for some of their sins. Of men many are trespassers.

1007. **Q: In 3:61 what does the Quran say about liars in relation to Jesus?**

A: To those who argue with you about him (Jesus) after the knowledge that has come to you say, "Come, let us call our children and your children, our women and your women, ourselves and yourselves, then call upon Allah to let His curse falls upon the Liars."

1008. **Q: Give an example of a hypocrite's behaviour according to 59:11–12.**

A: Have you seen the hypocrite telling their companions from those who deny of the people of the book, "If you are driven out, we shall go out with you and we obey no orders from anyone against you, and if you are fought with, we shall support you, and Allah witnesses that they are liars."

If they are driven out, they will not go out with them, if they are fought with they will not support them and if they do, they will turn in flight, then they shall not be delivered.

1009. **Q: In 3:92 how do you attain benevolence?**

A: You do not attain benevolence, until you give of what you love.

1010. **Q: Will Allah forgive those who deny his messenger?**

A: 9:80 said plead forgiveness for them or do not plead for them seventy times, Allah will not forgive them. This is because they have denied Allah and his messenger and Allah do not guild trespassers.

1011. **Q: What does 9:84 say about hypocrites?**

A: Do not pray over any of them ever or stand upon his grave. (This refers to hypocrites)

1012. **Q: What happens to liars according to 24:11?**

A: Those who have fabricated the lie are a group among you. Do not think it is an evil, but a good thing for you. For each of them have his share of sin. And for him who has undertaken the greater part of it, there is great torture.

1013. **Q: What did 9:107–108 say about mosques?**

A: And those who built a mosque for mischief, denial and separation between those who believe and watching for the arrival of him who

318

has fought Allah, and his messenger before. They will swear, "We sought only the good."

And Allah witnesses that they are liars. Do not ever pray in it.

A Mosque founded on piety from the first day is worthier of your prayers in it. There are men in it who love to purify themselves and Allah loves those who purify themselves.

1014. **Q: What did the Quran say must be done to polytheists?**

A: Should any of the polytheists ask your protection, give it to him, so that he may hear the word of Allah, then deliver him to where he feels safe. This is because: they are people we do not know.

1015. **Q: What does the Quran say about alcohol and gambling?**

A: In 5:90–91 – quotes, "O ye believe!

"Alcohol, gambling, idols set up and arrows for divination are filth of the devils doing.

"So, avoid them purchase you succeed. For the devil seeks to ease the enmity and loathing between you in gambling and alcohol and to divert you from remembering Allah and from prayers. So, will you be finished with them?"

1016. **Q: Does Allah allow innocents who are provoked to fight back?**

A: 22:39–40 – Permission is given to those who were attacked. For they were wronged. Allah can give them victory. Those who were driven out of their homes unfairly only because they said, "Our Lord is Allah."

NB: Islam is based upon justice and mercy and it abhors aggressiveness.

But the above verse gives permission only to those who were wronged.

1017. **Q: Does Allah allow people to fight in his name?**

A: 2:190 – Fight for Allah's sake those who fight you, but don't be the aggressors.

Allah does not like aggressors.

22:40 – Allah will support those who support him. Allah is the almighty, the invincible.

1018. **Q: When Islam goes to war and kill the enemies, who does the killing?**

A: 8:17 – You did not kill them but Allah kills them. You did not throw but Allah threw.

NB: this was said after the battle of Medina.

1019. **Q: What happens to false witnesses?**

A: 17:81 – And say, "The truth has come and the false has perished away. The false always perishes."

1020. **Q: Will God forgive sinners?**

A: In the Quran 7:56 it says the mercy of the Allah is close by the gracious. And in 6:54 – When those who believe our words come to you, say, "Peace be upon you." Your Lord has undertaken mercy upon himself. If any of you does wrong in ignorance, then repents after it and reforms. He is the merciful, the forgiving.

1021. **Q: According to the Quran 3:144 who was/is Muhammad?**

A: Muhammad is only a messenger whom other messengers have preceded, should he die or get killed, would you turn your heels? He who turns on his heels shall not harm Allah in the least and Allah will reward the thankful.

1022. **Q: What might happen to unbelievers according to 26:3–4?**

A: Perchance you will destroy yourself lest they do not believe, should we wish it, we could send down a token from heaven that would keep their necks bent in submission.

1023. **Q: Where in the Quran does it confirm that the Quran is completed?**

A: 5:3 Prophet Muhammed (Phub) said "Today, I have completed your religion, completed bestowing my blessing upon you and approved Islam as a religion for you".

6:38 – And we have neglected nothing in the book.

1024. **Q: Did Muhammad have dreams or visions?**

A: Of course – that was how the content of the Quran was revealed to him.

Visions and dreams are part of a prophet's life (prophesy).

It is also interesting to know that the Quran Chapters 16, line 89 stated:

"This book I am sending you down is clarification of Everything."

It is very important to know that the Angel told Joseph and Mary to take baby Jesus to Egypt where they stayed until King Herod died, when Jesus was 10-years-old. I am not surprised as some Muslims think that Jesus was brought up as a Muslim.

There was no Christianity or Islam then. Both the Muslims and Christians protect the so-called Moses Law, but some use it to justify their way.

When Moses said if someone slaps you, slap him back or you can marry your brother's widow, or divorce and marry, etc. All these were said because the Jews put pressure on him and with Moses' temper he gave in for what they wanted to hear.

1025. **Q: Muslim and Christian for about 75% of the world religious faith. There has been** argument about who is greater; Prophet Muhammad or Jesus Christ?

A: Jesus and Muhammad (Pbuh) were God's/ Allah's special messengers with special revelation to the world and they are both equal.

1026. **Q: What does the Quran say about greater prophet Jesus, Muhammad and others?**

A: In Surah 3:84, the Quran said "We believe in God, and in the revelation given to us, and to Ibrahim (Abraham), Ishmael, Isaac, Jacobs and the tribes. We believe in all that was given to Moses (Ten Commandments) Jesus and all the other messengers from the Lord we make no distinction between them. To God alone we surrender.

1027. **Q: Do Muslims believe Jesus to be the Son of God?**

A: No.

1028. **Q: If Jesus was not the Son of God why do Muslims respect him so much?**

A: Muslims agree with Christians and some other religious faith that Jesus possessed special or unique characteristics which includes:

He was born of a virgin.

Born and practiced God's will.

He healed many people physically, mentally and psychologically.

He was able to intervene with laws of nature.

Raised the dead all by God's will.

1029. **Q: How do Muslims regard the path or way to God/Allah?**

A: This is answered in the Quran (Surah 1:6-7) "show us the straightway, the way of those on whom You have bestowed Your grace, whose portion is not wrath, and who do not go astray".

1030. **Q: Is there anywhere else in the Quran about the Path to God/ Allah?**

A: According to Quran (Surah 6:53)

"This is my straight path, so follow it and do not follow the path which will separate you from it"

Also see Surah 57:28.

1031. **Q: Do Muslims believe the Nicene Creed 325 CE)**

A: Muslims believe Jesus was born by Virgin Mary but do not believe that Jesus was incarnated of God. Therefore, Muslims do not believe Jesus was "uncreated", God Himself, begotten and not made, being of one substance with the Father. It must be emphases that not all Christians believe Jesus as God, the cross is Jesus has attributes of God which made him special.

1032. **Q: What evidence supports Muslims that Jesus was not God?**

A: According to the Bible (Matthew 4:1-10): Jesus after 40 days fasting, when Satan tempted him, he said to Satan, "Begone, Satan! For it is written. 'You shall worship your Lord your God and Him only shall you serve.'"

1033. **Q: Is there more evidence Jesus was not God?**

A: The disciples asked Jesus how to teach them how to pray he taught them, "Our Father who art in heaven." This confirms that we are all children of God.

1034. **Q: What other evidence is there that interpretation might be difficult for Muslims and Christians to live in harmony?**

A: With the Quran, one does not need interpretation, in that what one reads what is the real message.

The Bible New Testament is a biography of Jesus whose teaching includes parables and gives rise to people in different interpretations.

Refer to St. John 14:16, Jesus was reported to have said, "I am, the way, the truth and the life. No one comes to the Father but by me."

1035. **Q: What was the meaning of when Jesus stated that he is the word?**

A: The meaning of this verse was that Jesus' teaching was the Word and if one does not follow what he was teaching, then it would be difficult to go to the Father. The statement could apply to any messenger of God who is teaching or revealing God's word. For example, Prophet

Muhammad, Lord Krishna, Guru Nanak, etc. could also have use these sentences or statements.

1036. **Q: What does it really mean when in St. John 10:38 Jesus said, "I and my Father are one."**

A: Here, Jesus was telling the people that His teaching was consistent with the Almighty God. Similarly, other prophets could use the same phrase. For example, the revelation of the 10 Commandments to Moses (which is in the Quran), the revelation of the Quran to Prophet Muhammad, the revelation of the Psalms (which are scattered in the Quran) to David. All of them were gods and hence, God and "named prophet" are one.

1037. **Q: How does one know Jesus was not God?**

A: In St. John 17:23 it says, "He who believes in me believes not in me but in Him who sent me." This is clear that Jesus was a messenger.

1038. **Q: How is eternal life portrayed in the Christian world?**

A: Refer to St. John 17:3, Jesus said, "That they know thee, the only one true God and Jesus whom thou has sent."

1039. **Q: What did St. James 2:19 say about God?**

A: You believe that God is one? You do well. Even the demons and shudder.

Forgiveness

1040. **Q: Considering the strict laws of Islam, for example, chopping the hand of a robber, capital punishment for rapists and eating pig not being accepted. Does this mean there is no forgiveness in the Quran?**

A: The Quran stated clearly that God has abundant mercy.

In Surah 39:53, "O my servant, who has transgressed against their souls? Do not despair of the mercy of God for He forgives ALL SINS, He is forgiving, most merciful.

1041. **Q: What did the devil promised to do?**

A: According to Ahmad, Prophet Muhammad quoted from the devil or Satan, who said, "By my honour, O Lord, I shall never stop misguiding your servants so long as life remains in their bodies. God was reported to have said, "By My honour, I shall never cease forgiving them, so long as they ask forgiveness of me."

Also, Surah 16:61 emphasises God's forgiveness, also in Hadiths and Hadith Quds.

1042. **Q: We all accept the Quran was a miracle spanning over 23 year's revelations to Prophet Muhammad. Why didn't the prophet perform miracles when asked?**

A: The Quran (Surah 17:90-93) said, "Say My Lord is high above these things. I am only a man and His messenger.

1043. **Q: All religion, including Islam, agree that Jesus' special gift from God was to perform miracles. Why didn't Prophet Muhammad claim the same?**

A: The Quran (Surah 7: 188) states, "I have no control over what may be helpful to me or hurtful to me, but as Allah wills. Had I the full knowledge of the unseen, I should increase my good, and evil should not touch me. (But) I am only a warner, an announcer of good things to those who believe.

1044. **Q: What did the Quran (Surah 109) say about other faith who did not believe in the Quran?**

A: "Say: O ye who do not believe, I do not worship that which you worship, and you will not worship that which I worship. And I will not worship that which you have always been used to worship, nor will you worship what I worship. To be your way, and to be mine."

1045. **Q: What is the mission statement of the Islamic faith?**

A: "La ilaha ilallah WA Muhammad ur-rasul ullah."

1046. **Q: There is no other God but Allah (the one) and Muhammad is the prophet of Allah.**

A: I believe in Allah, in His angels, in His revealed books, in all His prophets, in the Day of Judgement, in that everything both good and evil – comes from Him, and in life after death.

1047. **Q: What are the five Classical Arguments first introduced in the Middle Age by St. Thomas**

Aquinas (Christian) and Ibn al- Arabi (Muslims)?

A:

a. Design known as teleological argument.

b. Necessary being called ontological argument.

c. Contingency that did not exist.

d. First movement initiates action.

e. First cause – there must be a cause for something to happen.

1048. **Q: What part does nature play in God?**

A: God created nature, but humans created images to present things that have demons of power. People turn to associate things or living things with God. The Quran said, "Nothing is like unto Him."

1049. **Q: Approximately how many beautiful names are attributed to God in the Quran and please name a few?**

A: There are about 100 names, but some scholars think there are more than 100. Some of the names for are God are:

a. Source of peace (as Salam).

b. The Bestower (al-Wahhab).

c. All seeing (al-Basir).

d. The Protecting friend (al-Wali).

e. Pardoner (al-Afuw).

f. The Avenger (al-Muntagin).

g. Annihilator (al-Muni).

h. Preventer (al-Mani).

i. Abaser (al-Khalid).

Angels

1050. **Q: Do Islam believe in Angels?**

A: Yes, Islam believe that angels are in the whole universe.

They also believe that everyone has at least two angels (one records good and bad things about individuals) due to God forgiving upon repentance, there are more good records since repentance wipes all the sin away.

1051. **Q: Do Angels (Jinn's) believe that Arch angels have specific angels and please name some?**

A: Yes, Muslims believe in functions, for example: Gabriel (Jibreel) the head of messenger of God; (2) Michael (Mikail) the guardian of Holy places; (3) Azrail – the angel of death; (4) Israfil – will announce the judgement day; and (5) Munkir and Nakir – to question the soul of newly dead.

1052. **Q: Give Quran quotations about Angels**

A: In the Quran 41:30-32, Angels said to believers and believe in the good news about the state of Paradise which you have been promised. We are your protecting friends, in the life of this world and in the next.

1053. **Q: Who is the evillest spirit?**

A: Satan or Shaytan

1054. **Q: Name the Holy books of God and who they were revealed to?**

A:

a. The Quran to Muhammad.

b. Ten Commandments to Moses (Musa).

c. Psalms to David (Dawud).

d. Wisdom to Solomon (Sulayman).

e. Gospel of Jesus Injil (Evangel).

1055. **Q: What or who are messengers?**

A: In Surah 14:4, 25:51, 35:24 are some messengers. There are no people, but we have sent them a warner.

1056. **Q: How many messengers were mentioned in the Quran and name Major Prophets?**

A: 25 were mentioned in the Quran. The Major Prophets include Noah (Nuh), Abraham (Ibrahim), Moses (Musa), Solomon (Sulayman), Jesus (Isa) and Muhammad.

1057. **Q: How many were there and name these messengers mention in Quran but not in Bible.**

A: There are three namely: Hud Salih and Shay.

1058. **Q: List the prophets mentioned in both the Quran and the Bible in order of birth.**

A: Adam, Enoch (Idris), Noah (Nuh), Abraham (Ibrahim), Ishmael (Ismall), Isaac (Ishaa), Jacob (Yaqub), Joseph (Yusuf), Job (Ayyub), Moses (Musa), Aaron (Harum), Ezekiel (Dhulfik), David (Dawuel), Solomon (Sulayman), Elya (Ilyas) Elisha (Al-Yasa), Jonah (Yunus), Zukaria

(Zakary), John the Baptist (Yahya), Jesus (Isa) and Muhammad.

1059. **Q: In Islam what is "barzakh"?**

A: The waiting period that comes between the physical death and resurrection.

1060. **Q: What is Muslim view about resurrection?**

A: In al-Qiyamah 75:4: "He (God) will restore us even to our fingerprints."

1061. **Q: What do Muslims call Heaven and Hell?**

A: Heaven – Jannah or Paradise.

Hell is called Jahannam.

1062. **Q: Does God know everything that happens to us?**

A: Yes; see Surah 6:17: "O Allah, whatever you want to give me, no one can stop it from coming to me, and whatever You want to prevent from coming to me, nobody can give it to me."

1063. **Q: Explain Sunni Muslims?**

A: Sunni is the largest about 90% of Islam/Muslim they are orthodox Muslim. This sect is where the Prophet Muhammad belonged.

1064. **Q: What is Shia Muslim?**

A: This sect believes that the Prophet's son-in-law Ali should have succeeded the Prophet.

Inheritance in The Quran

1065. **Q: Give six inheritances in the Quran**

A:

a. Surah Maidah Chapter 5 verse 106-108.

b. Surah Nisa Chapter 4 verse 33.

c. Surah Nisa Chapter 4 verse 19.
    Surah Nisa Chapter 4 verse 7–9.

d. Surah Baqarah Chapter 2 verse 2406.

e. Surah Baqarah Chapter 2 verse 180.

f. The Quran gives guidance of how to share inheritance. These can be found in Chapter 4 verse 11, 12, 176.

1066. **Q: What advice does the Quran give about those who ask questions about legal decisions regarding partners' separation?**

A: Al-Quran 4:176: "They ask you for legal decision, say Allah directs (them) about those who leave no descendants on ascendants as heirs. If it is a man that dies, leaving a sister no descendants or ascendants as heirs. If it is a man that dies leaving a sister but no child, her brother takes her inheritance, if there are two sisters, they shall have two thirds of the inheritance (between them). If there are brothers and sisters (they share), the male having twice the share of the female. This dies Allah make clean to you (His knowledge of all things)."

In what your wives leave, your share is half. If they have no child; if they leave a child, you get a fourth after the payment of legacies and debts. Al-Quran 4:11-12.

JESUS AND IBRAHIM

1067. **Q: What was Jesus' religion?**

A: In Al-Quran 52 verse 3 Jesus was a Muslim.

1068. **Q: What was Abraham's religion?**

A: According to Al-Quran 67:3 Ibrahim (Abraham) was not a Jew but a Muslim.

1069. **Q: Does the Quran allow division such as sects?**

A: As for those who divide their religion and break up into sects, thou hast no part in them in the least. Their affair is within Allah: He will in the end tell them the truth of all that they did (Al-Quran 6:159).

1070. **Q: Why do people call themselves Muslims?**

A: Surah Fissile Chapter 41 verse 33 says if you are asked, be pleased to say, "I am a Muslim, not a Hanafi or a Shafi."

Who is better in speech than one who calls (men) to Allah works righteousness and says, "I am of those who bow in Islam (Muslim)" Al-Quran 41:33.

1071. **Q: It is believed that Prophet Muhammad dictated a letter inviting kings and dignity to join Islam, where is this in the Quran?**

A: Quran Surah Ali Imran Chapter 3 verse 64 says, "Bear witness that we (at least) are Muslims (bowing to Allah's will)."

1072. **Q: What punishment is there for the one who is a convicted robber?**

A: Al-Quran 5:38: "As to the thief, male or female, out of his hands: a punishment by way of example, from Allah is exalted in power full of wisdom."

1073. **Q: Why are people afraid to talk about Islam?**

A: This should not be if the non-Muslim really wants to learn, but if he mocks Islam then the consequence is unpredictable. This is one lesson I learnt when I was doing my research for my books. The Quran says, "Ah! Who is more unjust than those who conceal the testimony they have from Allah? But Allah is not unmindful of what you do!" (Al-Quran 2:140)

In Al-Quran 16:125: "Invite (all) to the way of your Lord, with wisdom and beautiful preaching, and argue with them in ways that are best and most gracious."

1074. **Q: What are the five categories of Do's and Don'ts?**

A:

a. Haram – prohibited or forbidden.

b. Makrut – not recommended or discourage.

c. Mumba – permissible or allowed.

d. Mustahab – recommended or encouraged.

e. Fard – compulsory or obligatory.

1075. **Q: Does the Quran allow Muslims to eat non-vegetable foods?**

A: Yes, the Quran permits Muslims to eat non-vegetable food, for example, Al-Quran 23:21: "And in cattle (too) you have an instructive example: From within their bodies we produce (milk) for you to drink; there are in them (besides) numerous (other) benefits for you, and of their meat you eat."

"Cattle He has created for you (men) from them you derive warmth, and numerous benefits, and of their meat you eat." Al-Quran 16:5

In Al-Quran 5:1: "O you who believe! Fulfil (all) obligations. Lawful unto you (for food) are all four-footed animals with the exceptions named."

1076. **Q: Does the Quran prohibit non-vegetables?**

A: The Quran allows only herbivorous animals.

1077. **Q: Please quote from the Quran what animals prohibit?**

A: In Al-Quran 59:7: "So take what the messenger assigns to you and deny yourselves that which he withholds from you."

In Al-Quran 7:157 the prophet commends them what is just and prohibits what is evil. He (Allah) allows them as lawful what is good (and pure) and prohibits them what is bad and impure.

1078. **Q: Where can we find Prophet Muhammad (Pbuh) being prohibited from eating carnivorous animals?**

A: In the book of hunting and slaughter. Hadith No 4752, Hadith No 3232 to 3234, Sunan Ibn-I-Majah chapter 13.

1079. **Q: What type of carnivorous animals does the prophet prohibit?**

A:

a. Wild animals with canine teeth, including: cats, lions, tigers, dogs, wolves and hyenas.

b. Rodents: mice, rats and rabbits with claws.

c. Some reptiles like snakes and alligators.

d. Birds of prey – vultures, eagle, crows and owls.

1080. **Q: Muslims turn their face towards Ka'ba during prayers, does it mean they worship it?**

A: No, Muslims (Islam) only worship one Allah the Al-Quran 2:144 says, "We see the turning of your face (for guidance) to the heavens: now shall we turn you to a Qiblah that shall please you. Turn then your face in the direction of the Sacred Mosque: wherever you are, turn your faces in that direction."

1081. **Q: What is black-stone attributed?**

A: Black-stone (Hajr-e-aswad) is traditionally attributed to the Prophet's long-time companion Umar (Pbuh) who is reported to have said, "I know that you are a stone and can neither benefit nor harm. Had I not seen the Prophet (Pbuh) touching and kissing you, I would never have touched and kissed you."

1082. **Q: Where in the Quran does it state two female witnesses are equal to one male in a financial transaction?**

A: Al-Quran 2:282: "O you who believe! When you deal with each other in transactions involving future obligation in a fixed period reduce them to writing and get two witness out of your own men and if there are not two men then a man and two women, such as you choose for witnesses so that if one of them errs the other can remind her."

1083. **Q: What does err mean?**

A: Err in Quran is Tazil which means confused or err.

1084. **Q: What verse in the Quran supports equality, i.e. one male equal one female in financial affairs?**

A: In Surah Noor Chapter 24:6 (Al-Quran 24:6): "And those who launch a charge against their spouses and have (in support) no evidence but their own – their solitary evidence can be received."

1085. **Q: Which verse in the Quran talks about Final Judgement?**

A: Al-Quran 3:185: "Every soul shall have a taste of death and only on the Day of Judgement shall you be paid your full recompense. Only he who is saved far from the fire and admitted to the garden will have attained the object (of life) for the life of this world is but goods and chattels of deception."

1086. Q: What did the Quran say about very evil people like Hitler?

A: In Al-Quran 4:56: "Those who reject our signs, we shall soon cast into the fire; as often as their skins are roasted through, we shall change them for fresh skins that may taste the penalty: for Allah is exalted in power-wise."

1087. Q: Which part in the Quran supports UNITY?

A: Islam like most religious faiths is divided, but the Quran advocate Unity. In Al-Quran 6:159: "As for those who divide their religion and break up into sects, thou hast no part in them in the least: Their affair is with Allah. He will in the end tell them the truth of all that they did."

1088. Q: What are some of the divisions in Islam?

A: Sunni, Shia, Hanafi, Shafi, Maliki, Humbali and Deobandi Barelui.

1089. Q: What did Prophet Muhammad say about the 73 different sects of Islam?

A: Referring to Timidhi Hadith No. 171, Prophet Muhammad is reported to have said that all the 73 sects would be in Hell fire except for he said, "It is the one to which I and my companions belong."

1090. **Q: Did prophet Muhammad predict the split in Islam?**

A: From Sunan Abu Dawood Hadith No. 4579 Prophet Muhammad was reported to have said, "My community will be split up into seventy-three sects."

1091. **Q: What is Zakat and what does it demand?**

A: Zakat is an obligatory annual charity by Islamic law. That any Islam whose savings exceed the equivalent to 85 grams of gold he or she must give 2.5% every lunar year in charity.

It has been said that Islam advocates killing innocent civilians who do not agree to this.

The presumption is not true: the Islam community in Birmingham, England, etc. openly detest this accusation. A quotation from the Quran in support of preservation of human life especially the civilian Al-Quran 5:32 says, "...To kill an innocent person is like killing the whole of mankind likewise if one saves mankind it is like saving the life of all mankind." Also refer to Al-Quran 60:8 "... Allah loves those who deal with equality."

1092. **Q: What about Islam killing in the event of war?**

A: This question must also be answered by all faiths or politicians when lawful war is declared between nations. It is acceptable to kill to win. Referring to some God messengers such as Lord Krishna, Vishnu, Ganesh, Siva (Hindus) etc. all went to war.

Prophet Muhammad was no exception. The Quran Al-Quran 4:75 supported killing in the event of lawful war: "...Why should you not fight in the cause of God and those who being weak, are ill-treated men, women and children whose cry is '...Our Lord (Allah) rescue us from this town whose people are oppressors, ... arise for us from the one who will help.'"

We must remember that Islam means peace, NO, they do NOT support torture, or killing by false pretences.

1093. **Q: There have been outcries of suicide bombing, what is Islam's view on this?**

A: The term suicide bombing is modern terminology. The fact is that there are many verses in the Quran which forbids killing of innocent people and the majority of Muslims distance themselves from this outrageous behaviour of less than one percent of Muslims.

In fact, one scholar, Shaykh al-Uthaymeen, is reported to have said, "Indeed my opinion is that he (suicide bomber) is regarded as one who has killed himself and as a result he shall be punished in Hell."

Furthermore, Prophet Muhammad (Pbuh) is reported to have said, "Indeed, whoever kills himself intentionally will be punished in the fire of Hell wherein he shall dwell forever."

1094. **Q: Is it advocating that Islam force people to join their religion?**

348

A: In fact, there was a lot of these Eastern countries – India notable Guru Nanak (a Sikh teacher) four boys who were killed and eventually himself for failing to join or change his belief to Islam.

Most modern Muslims I researched denied this and in fact do not agree to the historical torture of people to join Islam. Quran al-Quran 2:256 said, "Let there be no compulsion in religion."

1095. **Q: The term Muslim extremist has been used to describe a small minority who torture, discriminate and kill innocent people. What does the Quran say about this?**

A: The text in the Quran and what Prophet Muhammad (Pbuh) was reported to have said was to forbid all forms of extremism or terrorism.

1096. **Q: Do Muslims support faith unity?**

A: Yes, al-Quran 49:13: "O mankind we created you from a single pair of male and female, and made you know each other. Verily the most honoured of you in the sight of God is he who is

349

the most righteous of you. And God has full knowledge, and all is well-acquainted with all things.

Chapter 8

Jainism

1097. **Q: Whose teaching resulted in Jainism and when did he live?**

A: Vardhamana Mahavira 599 to 527BC.

1098. **Q: Who was he?**

A: He renounced his prince-hood and wealth and became a monk.

1099. **Q: What other faith leaders renounced their prince-hoods?**

A: Buddha left the palace and renounced his prince-hood; he took a bowl and became a monk for six years.

1100. **Q: What does Jainism mean?**

A: Jainism comes from Jina (which means Victor or Conqueror) and stands for someone who has achieved the highest spiritual freedom.

1101. **Q: What names are given to the prophet and first and last?**

A: Tirthankaras means prophet. The first was Tirthankar Rishabhdev (initiator) and the last Mahavira being the last of 24 prophets.

1102. **Q: What do they believe?**

A: There is no creator, saviour or destroyer and no supreme power to give pain or joy.

1103. **Q: So why is it a religion?**

A: They believe in one shape the future of right deeds. That Thirthankaras (prophet) are gods.

1104. **Q: What is the teaching?**

A: Right belief, right knowledge and right conduct which are regarded as three jewels of religion guiding people to literation (Moksha).

1105. **Q: How do they consider the universe?**

A: It is made of infinite souls affected by Karma and a continued circle of reincarnation.

1106. **Q: What can the soul obtain?**

A: Freedom from the Karmic.

1107. **Q: What are the main principles of Jainism?**

A: Non-violence or Ahinsa, harmlessness to all living beings on the universe, truthfulness, no stealing, sexual restraint and self-control (Sanyam) in speech, action, thoughts.

1108. **Q: Are there any diet restrictions?**

A: They are strict vegetarians – no eggs, fish, onion, potatoes, root crops, garlic, carrot. Apart from milk and milk products all food with animal sources are forbidden. No food or drink after sunset.

1109. **Q: How do they worship?**

A: By visiting the temple for worship known as Puja.

1110. **Q: Are there any festivals?**

A: These are connected to the Prophet (Tirthankara's life), i.e. descended from Heaven, birth, renunciation, attainment of omniscience, death and final emancipation.

1111. **Q: Who performs marriage ceremonies?**

A: A Hindu priest known as Brahmin.

1112. **Q: Which religion do they identify themselves with?**

A: Hindus.

1113. **Q: Name their main religion.**

A:

a. Samvatsary – the final day of Paryushana Fast.

b. Mahavira Janma Halyanak – the birthday of Lord Mahavira (March/April).

c. Diwali – to celebrate qualification as Moksha or enlightenment and it is the last day of the year.

d. New Year is the day after Diwali.

1114. **Q: Do they fast?**

A: Eight day fasting (August/September).

1115. **Q: Are there any dress restrictions?**

A: There are no restrictions. A woman may wear a Bindi on the forehead and Mangal Sutra around the neck.

1116. **Q: What happens to their dead?**

A: All are cremated.

1117. **Q: Who and when was Jainism formed?**

A: It was formed in 599–527BC by Jina popularly known as Conqueror (in India Ganges).

1118. **Q: What is the name of the last Jains?**

A: Mahavira.

1119. **Q: What do Jains believe?**

A: That the universe is subjected to growth and decline and that everyone needs to struggle to be free.

1120. **Q: What are the two main divisions of Jainism and how can you differentiate them?**

A: The monks who wear white robes are called "Svetamabaras" known as white clad. Digambaras monks show their renunciation of the world by being naked and are known as sky clad.

1121. **Q: What are their main laws?**

A: There must be no violence to any human or animals, hence they are vegetarian (never take away life).

1122. **Q: To avoid violence to insert on their walk path what characteristics to they show?**

A: Some nuns and monks sweep the path ahead as they walk, they even wear masks and serve the drinking water.

1123. **Q: What is their main philosophy?**

A: That human actions produce a force known as "Karma" the good actions.

1124. **Q: What do Jains regard as a bad action?**

A: Bad behaviour is an energy called fire or heat (tapas).

1125. **Q: What happens when one's soul is eventually free?**

A: The soul is called jiva, it then rises and lives in the summit of cosmos (nirvana).

1126. **Q: What is their greatest festival?**

A: It is called Pasryushana – during the Lord Mahavira's birthday in April or during the monsoon. They fast for at least eight days.

1127. **Q: What was the population in the year 20000?**

A: Seven million worldwide.

1128. **Q: What are the three jewels that Jains follow?**

A: Right knowledge, right faith and right conduct.

1129. **Q: What do Monks and Nuns do?**

A: They are religious teachers.

1130. **Q: What extra rules are there for monks and nuns?**

A: Right penance.

1131. **Q: What are the Great Vows of monks and nuns?**

A:

a. Non-violence

b. Speaking the truth

c. Sexual abstinence

d. Not taking what is not given

e. Detachment from people, places and things.

1132. **Q: What is another vow?**

A: They are to spend at least 48 minutes every day meditating.

1133. **Q: What extreme can monks or nuns go to?**

A: Only eat leftovers.

1134. **Q: What some ethics?**

A: That all things (breathing or not) are alive, including earth and metals.

1135. **Q: Are Jains allowed to do any occupation they like and why?**

A: No, such as cultivating harms creatures and the soil itself. Carpeting as sawing timber causes harm to it.

1136. **Q: What else do they avoid due to non-violence?**

A: They are not to sweep insects from the path, nor to strain drinking water to avoid the organism within, nor to use lamps so that moths do not perish in the flames and to wear face masks to prevent breathing in insects.

1137. **Q: What about fasting?**

A: Yes, during monthly full moon, eight days during the festival of Paryushana Parva (August).

Chapter 9

Judaism

1138. Q: What do we mean by anti-Semitism?

A: This term was used in the nineteenth century for the hostility, prejudice and persecution of the Jews.

1139. Q: What is the language and meaning of apocalypse?

A: It is a Greek word to mean Revelation which focuses on the Judgement day.

1140. Q: What is the Ark of the Covenant?

A: It is the Ark that contained the Ten Commandment tablets and is regarded as Holy.

1141. Q: What word in Hebrew is to mean we have sin?

A: Ashamnu.

1142. Q: Who are regarded as black Jews?

A: The Jewish congregation from Afro-Americans.

1143. **Q: What is blasphemy and the consequences?**

A: Speaking bad against God. The punishment is death (Leviticus 24:10–23).

1144. **Q: What is the difference between the book of life and the book of the Covenant, Book of Death?**

A: The book of life stands for God written the names of the righteous, whilst the book of death stands for the wicked and evil people. Book of the Covenant: The laws from God through Moses also known as laws of Exodus (Exodus 20:20–23, 33).

1145. **Q: What does the book of covenant cover?**

A: Mainly legislation on idolatry, charity, capital punishment and slavery.

1146. **Q: When can the Capital Punishment be invoked?**

A: For murder, adultery, sexual crimes, witchcraft, kidnapping and blasphemy.

1147. **Q: How far does once trace the history of Judaism?**

A: In Mesopotamia along the rivers of Tigris and Euphrates.

1148. **Q: Which religion was affected by the culture of Mesopotamia?**

A: The Hebrew religion.

1149. **Q: What did they use to write on?**

A: On stone and clay tablets.

1150. **Q: When did the Jews originate from?**

A: In the nineteenth and sixteenth centuries BCE.

1151. **Q: Who were believed to be the founders or pillars in which the Jewish developed?**

A: Abraham and his ancestors – Isaac and Jacob, etc.

1152. **Q: What was the land God promised the Jews?**

A: Canaan.

1153. **Q: Name two culture groups believed to originate the Jews.**

A: Semitic people from the North West and the semi-nomadic.

1154. **Q: Which Israelite two tribes united under King David?**

A: The Ephraim in the north and Judah from the south.

1155. **Q: Which king allowed the Jews to return to Jerusalem after being conquered by Babylonia?**

A: King Cyrus of Persia.

1156. **Q: Name the two traditions of Jews.**

A: Scribes and Pharisees.

1157. **Q: How were the Jews united?**

A: Their respect of the common heritage includes the Laws or Torah including the 10 Commandments, common tradition and liturgy.

1158. **Q: After Christ what happened to the Jews living with Muslims and Christians?**

A: The Jews became the minority and were commonly persecuted.

1159. **Q: What do they regard themselves as?**

A: As God's chosen people and God gave them the Holy book, *Torah* or the five books of the Old Testament.

1160. **Q: What did Moses get for them?**

A: God revealed the Ten Commandments and the laws to their leader Moses on Mount Sinai in 1200BCE.

1161. **Q: What is the Ark?**

A: The Ark contains the two tablets, which were inscribed with the Ten Commandments (it is the holiest sanctuary).

1162. **Q: Where was the Ark placed?**

A: In the King Solomon Temple (tenth century BCE), in Jerusalem (950BCE).

1163. **Q: Who are Rabbis?**

A: They are Jewish leaders in worshipping (Priest or Teachers).

1164. **Q: What is the name of the Judaism Holy book?**

A: Pentateuch (five books of the Old Testament) or *Torah* – Genesis, Exodus, Leviticus, Numbers and Deuteronomy.

1165. **Q: Who and when was King Solomon destroyed?**

A: By the Babylonians in 587BCE.

1166. **Q: When and by whom built the second temple?**

A: Zerubbabel rebuilt it in 516BC.

1167. **Q: When was the second temple destroyed and by whom?**

A: In 70CE by the Romans.

1168. **Q: When the synagogue was destroyed, what was the name of the structure and wall left standing and its significance?**

A: The wall and structure left standing is called the Wailing or the Western and up to now formed the pilgrimage for prayers.

1169. **Q: Describe a typical synagogue.**

A: The fronts have a Jewish logo ✡ the entrance leads to the forecourt, which contain washing facilities (wash away sins) and another door leads to the main synagogue.

1170. **Q: Is any behaviour in the worshippers described as equal?**

A: All monotheists worships the same God.

1171. **Q: How many years did it take Jews from Egypt to Israel?**

A: about 40 years.

1172. **Q: Was there an opportunity breached?**

A: No as it had been an agreed tradition that the Orthodox synagogue separated males from females. All sit but are separated by a screen and the (priest) Rabbi sits facing the worshippers.

1173. **Q: How do they treat children in the synagogue?**

A: Like most worshipping houses. The children who the parents think may disrupt the service are accommodated in another room with another Rabbi.

1174. **Q: Why do Judaism worshippers face the direction of the Ark or Jerusalem?**

A: Because the Ark contains the *Torah* and behind it is the Parochet.

1175. **Q: Name some festivals and when.**

A: The Jewish use flexible timing or lunar. The four festivals to being the year are Rosh Hashana, Yom Kippur, Sukkot and Simchat Torah.

1176. **Q: Give a brief description of each.**

A:

a. Rosh Hashana is a two-day festival to welcome the New Year, leading to ten days of reflection and penitence and sounded the SHOEAR.

b. Yom Kippur: This includes the ten days' penitence. It is for spiritual renewal and marked with a day of fasting. Yom Kippur is a day of atonement.

c. Sukkot: booth or feast of the Tabernacles and is a week-long, it starts five days after Yom Kippur.

d. Simchat Torah is a celebration of the Torah.

1177. **Q: Name other festivals.**

A: Tisha B'Av known as Fast of AV. It is a day of fasting to mourn the destruction of the Temple by the Romans in 70CE.

1178. **Q: What binds all the Jews in the world?**

A: They all accept the Torah which are the first five books of the Old Testament, irrespective of any division or culture or country.

1179. **Q: List most of the principles of Judaism.**

A:

a. They believe in one God.

b. The creation of the world is recorded in the first chapter of the first book.

c. God gave the Torah to the Jewish people.

d. The Jewish religion is based on the laws that God gave to Moses which became oral law Talmud and codes of Jewish law.

e. The Sabbath are festival holidays and all weekday activities are not allowed.

f. Diets are very minor compared to their religion.

g. Jews must always be law abiding.

h. Qualities include: kindness, compassion to all people, especially to the vulnerable and elderly, and no discrimination.

i. All good deeds will be rewarded, and bad deeds punished.

1180. **Q: When is the Sabbath?**

A: It starts at sunset on Fridays to nightfall on Saturday and is holy, no work.

1181. **Q: What are the major festivals?**

A: Passover (March/April); Pentecost (May/June).

1182. **Q: When are they and what is the name of the New Year?**

A: Usually in September/October and it is called Rosh Hashana and normally apples and honey are eaten and Rams horn (shofar) is sounded in the morning.

1183. **Q: What is the Day of Atonement?**

A: September/October and is a solemn fasting day spent in prayers and reflection.

1184. **Q: What are Tabernacles?**

A: September/October – Jews eat their meals in a hut or booth.

1185. **Q: What do Jews regard as four species?**

A: Palm branch, three myrtle branches, two willow branches and citron.

1186. **Q: What happens on "The Eighth" day of solemn Assembly and Rejoicing of the law?**

A: September/October to conclude autumn festival.

1187. **Q: What is the Festival of Light?**

A: It is called Purim and celebrated as a carnival.

1188. Q: Are there any restrictions?

A: The orthodox men cover their heads with a skullcap and married women cover their heads.

Purim (February/March): a celebration called Carnival Festival to remember Esther victory on the king's steward Haman to save the Jews.

Shavuot (also known as Pentecost): this is after Passover to remember God's revelation of the Ten Commandments to Israel and the world (through Moses).

Tu Bishevat: a day allocated for the year of trees.

Hanukkah: called celebration of Light; it is eight days long to remember miracles of lamp oil lasting more than expected.

Pesach: this is the celebration of the Passover (escape of the Israelite slaves from Egypt).

1189. Q: What is the name of the traditional Judaism?

A: Orthodox.

1190. Q: What is the Orthodox tradition?

A: The Orthodox abide by the unchanging faith of Israel and respect the Rabbi and their interpretation of the Torah. They cover their heads all day.

1191. **Q: How many times do Jews pray?**

A: Three times (morning, afternoon and evening).

1192. **Q: How do Judaism's prepare for prayer?**

A: They wash and cover their heads – especially men, known as Kippa.

1193. **Q: What is the significance of food?**

A: Food is called Kosher (or Permitted) and must be prepared according to Jewish dietary laws.

1194. **Q: Has there been any reform of Judaism?**

A:

- Yes, especially in the Western world, e.g. Reform Judaism (Germany) in 1840, regard Judaism institutionalised and believe "Jews were no longer a nation but citizens of the state".

- Conservative Judaism – in 1840 stuck to historic Judaism and adopted truism.

- Reconstructionism – this started in the 1920s in the USA and they believed that Judaism was a religious civilisation and expressed their culture.

1195. **Q: What is the name of the texts in the Torah?**

A: They are referred to as Mishmah (sacred texts).

1196. **Q: How many versions are there?**

A: Two – Gemara: Palestinian and the Babylonian.

1197. **Q: What is Talmud?**

A: It is the written Torah for teaching referred to as Pentateuch.

1198. **Q: How many estimated followers are there?**

A: 20 million followers.

1199. **Q: What is the main language of the Jews?**

A: Hebrew – believed to be stated in the Bible and it is still the religion today.

Chapter 10

Paganism

1200. Q: Name the three principles of paganism.

A: Love for and kinship with nature, positive morality, recognition of the divine.

1201. Q: What does Pagan mean by love?

A: It refers to the life-force and its incarnation.

1202. Q: Explain morality in Pagan belief.

A: Individuals are responsible to develop their true self/nature in harmony and portray it to the outer community.

1203. Q: How is Paganism founded?

A: On deity manifest in nature.

1204. Q: How do Pagans view seasonal change?

A: The change of seasons is much like the wheel turning and is regarded as a mystery of the divine.

1205. Q: How do Pagans visualise God?

A: Pagans believe in many faces of God in response to the season mystery, which relates to the vision of God.

1206. **Q: Do Pagans celebrate seasons?**

A: Yes, seasons are sowing and reaping, from winter, spring, summer and autumn.

1207. **Q: How many festivals do Pagans have?**

A: There are many but eight are major.

1208. **Q: What are these seasonal linked to?**

A: These are linked to the four solar festivals by equinoxes and solstices.

1209. **Q: What are four Celtic festivals?**

A: The four are Imbolc, Beltane, Lughnasadh and Samhain.

1210. **Q: When is the Pagan New Year?**

A: Some Pagans regard Samhain or 31 sOctober as the Celtic New Year.

1211. **Q: What is significant of Yule?**

A: This is usually 21 sDecember and believed that the sun child is reborn symbolising new life in the name of the Gods.

1212. **Q: Who administers worship?**

A: Pagan substitution for priest is Wicca gothic who could be male or female.

1213. **Q: What is given to a female priest?**

A: Seidkona or volva.

1214. **Q: What is one of Pagans teachings?**

A: That the current problem in the world is due to forgotten wisdom of the past and that modern philosophy is changing attitude to the divine.

1215. **Q: How do Pagans know the truth?**

A: That the truth is revealed to individuals within us.

1216. **Q: How do we find the truth?**

A: Through meditation.

1217. **Q: What is the name of different Pagan religions?**

A: They are collectively known as tradition.

1218. **Q: Name two traditions.**

A: Druidry and Wicca.

1219. **Q: Which is the northern tradition?**

A: It is called Asatru or Odinism and regarded as German gods.

1220. **Q: Where is shamanism dominant?**

A: Mainly among some Europeans, Siberians and some Americans.

1221. **Q: Do they have a goddess group?**

A: Yes.

1222. **Q: Which countries does one find a goddess group?**

A: Greece and Rome have WICCA: some Egyptians also practice.

1223. **Q: Where are Paganism roots or practices?**

A: It is practiced within some religions in Europe, Africa, Japan, Afro-Caribbean and America.

1224. **Q: How is the ritual performed?**

A: It takes place in front of an altar placed in the north.

1225. **Q: How is the altar constructed?**

A: It is made of wood or stone.

1226. **Q: What do they have on the altar?**

A: There may be a statue of their gods or deity. Some might have objects as symbolisation.

1227. **Q: What other things do Pagans use in their rituals?**

A: Lighted candles and burning incense.

1228. **Q: Which festival is associated with Goddess?**

A: Ceremony of "Wine and Cake" which represents the body as blood and life (some use water).

1229. **Q: Name a few other things used in Pagan rituals?**

A: Feathers, seashells, stones, pictures, plants, flowers, bowl with water and salt, and tapes.

1230. **Q: What do Pagans do to the environment before the ritual beings?**

A: The place is purified using incense, perfumes, prayers, invocation and devotions with chanting.

1231. **Q: Quote one of the teachings.**

A: This quote is from a leaflet I was given during my research, "That in the darkest time, there is hope of another day, that in the time of suffering, we shall know release, that all beauty is transient, and though we honour it while it flowers, yet do we give greater honour to that which endures and abides love, honour, wisdom, truth, courage and compassion."

1232. **Q: What is the most important principle of Paganism?**

A: Most Pagans follow the slogan "Do what you will as long as it harms none".

1233. **Q: What do Pagan ethics depend on?**

A: They do not seek perfection but harmony and balance and most importantly not to harm anyone.

1234. **Q: What is normal ritual dress?**

A: Usually a long black hoodless robe but it could be any colour or material depending on the type of tradition one belongs to.

1235. **Q: What about their diet?**

A: Most Pagans are kind and love nature, so some are vegetarian, i.e. do what you will if it harms no one. Some are vegans.

1236. **Q: Does Britain recognise Pagan weddings?**

A: This is not formally legalised, so they must register after their ritual marriage.

1237. **Q: What happens when Pagans die?**

A: Pagans believe in reincarnation and they could either be cremated or buried.

Chapter 11

Shinto

1238. **Q: Where will you find the Shinto religion?**

A: Japan and China.

1239. **Q: What does Shinto mean?**

A: Spirits or gods (the Chinese call it shen tao).

1240. **Q: What is Shinto related to in Japan?**

A: Their practice relates to a shrine called Jinga.

1241. **Q: What do they call their sacred places relating to the shrine?**

A: Kami.

1242. **Q: How far back can history trace it?**

A: The sixth century CE.

1243. **Q: What other faiths does Shinto relate to?**

A: Buddhism historically and Confucianism.

1244. **Q: How is Shinto involved with two deities?**

A: Shinto derives sacred written scriptures, morality, personal and is possibly looked upon for salvation.

1245. **Q: What about Confucianism?**

A: Confucianism underpins the concept of sincerity, purity and socially acceptable ethics.

1246. **Q: Since they relate to the Chinese as well, what other faiths could it involve?**

A: Some of their beliefs are derived from Taoism (China).

1247. **Q: When did it change majorly?**

A: From 1868, new scholars got rid of the Buddhism element.

1248. **Q: Who do Shinto's devote to?**

A: Until the 1890s Shinto devotion was to the emperor.

1249. **Q: What happened after 1890?**

A: From 1890, it was declared as a "Non-religion" and the ritual relates to the emperor were believed to have been a descendant of the Sun Goddess, Amaterasu.

1250. **Q: If Shinto is non-religious how is the state of Japan related?**

A: In 1945 Shinto was enforced by the modern government and introduced to other religions in Japan (known as State Shinto).

1251. **Q: What happened to the emperor?**

A: The emperor renounced his claim of divinity in place to the Allied Occupation Powers and freedom of religion.

1252. **Q: What happened to the shrine?**

A: There are other sects who still have connections to the Shinto shrine and its deities.

1253. **Q: Describe a typical shrine.**

A: They are noticed by torti – large portals or upright crossbars pained red – but not always with running water supposed to be used as purification of hands and mouth before one approach "Kami" to worship.

1254. **Q: How do worshippers get to Kemi, to get to the most sacred place known as the residence of Kami?**

A: Some residences of Kami demand going through gates or bridges to cross as these shrines are the most sacred.

1255. **Q: What does one do as you worship?**

A: In most cases, you offer cash, clapping your hands and say your petition.

1256. **Q: How many shrines and Kami's are there in Japan?**

A: About 100,000 shrines and over 80 million Kami.

1257. **Q: Around 2000: how many followers were there?**

A: 100 million.

1258. **Q: Is Shinto the only faith?**

A: Not really; Shinto and Buddhism are practiced together in Japan.

Chapter 12

Sikhism

1259. Q: What makes Sikhs parallel with other major monotheists?

A: Their faith in "One God" who is infinite, spiritual. Their first most belief is love, which is the summary of the Ten Commandments.

1260. Q: What other faith makes Sikhs please God?

A: Harmony, equality, service to humans and charity.

1261. Q: When and who founded Sikhism?

A: Around the mid-fifteenth century by Guru Nanak Deo Ji who claimed to be a teacher of God's word to people. He was meek, never claimed to be special and he was not a messenger or a prophet.

1262. Q: What is the Holy scripture of Sikh called?

A: Sri Guru Granth Sahib Ji.

1263. Q: What name did they call God?

A: Wahe Guru, which means wonderful Lord.

1264. **Q: What is the name of the place of worship?**
A: Gurdwara.

1265. **Q: Where do Sikhs regard as their holy place where pilgrimage is encouraged?**
A: Sri Harmander Sahib popularly known as The Golden Temple in Amritsar in Panjab, India.

1266. **Q: What is Sikh's philosophy of faith?**
A: It is known as 5K's which are:

1. Kesh (uncut hair)

2. Kanga (comb)

3. Kara (steel bangle)

4. Kachh (special pair of shorts)

5. Kirpan (sword).

1267. **Q: What do these 5K's mean to Sikhs?**
A: It stands for Sikh's identity and Amritdhari. Sikhs wear these to mean humility, cleanliness, restraint, continence, dignity and respectfulness.

1268. **Q: How can one identify Sikh men?**
A: Men have nicely kept hair, beard and turban (which can be any colour: blue, white, black, red, or orange).

1269. **Q: How do you identify Sikh women?**

A: They use long scarves known as Dupatta over their hair.

1270. **Q: Which area is the most populated with Sikhs and how many are there in the world?**

A: Panjab in India is their homeland where about 12 million of 20 million people live.

1271. **Q: What is the language original to current?**

A: Sikh language is Panjabi, then was changed to Gurmukhi, derived from India script called Brahami.

1272. **Q: How would you describe a Sikh person?**

A: Sir Alexander Burnes sums this up as: "The Sikh nation is very large hearted. Despite racial differences, they co-exist with others happily and remain kind hearted."

1273. **Q: What are the popular greetings of Sikhs?**

A: Wahe guru Ji Ka Khalsa, Wahe guru Ji Ki Fateh (which means The Khalsa belongs to God, the victory belongs to God).

1274. **Q: What does "Sat sri Akal" mean?**

A: "Truth is God or God is Truth".

384

1275. **Q: What is the Sikh's popular festival?**

A: It is regarded as holy day known as Gurpurb.

1276. **Q: What is Nagar Keertan?**

A: It is dancing on the street in carnival mood.

1277. **Q: What is Palki?**

A: It is a decorative throne with Guru Granth Sahib Ji seated, and it can be carried or wheeled.

1278. **Q: What is the brotherhood of Sikhs?**

A: It is called Khalsa and represents the five symbols of their faith.

1279. **Q: Name the five symbols.**

A:

a. Kesh – uncut hair and beard

b. Kangha – comb to groom and fix the hair in place in the turban

c. Kara – circular steel wristband

d. Kirpan – miniature sword

e. Kach – knee-length shorts. The men must wear these for their faith. The Kara and Kirpan remind Sikhs of their responsibilities.

1280. **Q: What is the meaning of Guru?**

A: A religious leader who teaches and gives guidance to the Sikh.

1281. **Q: Who was the first leader and what was his philosophy?**

A: Guru Nanak. His philosophy was, "There is neither Hindu nor Muslim that is God is not interested in our religious label but in the way we conduct ourselves." He said, "All religion must be respected as we worship the same God."

1282. **Q: What did Guru Nanak say about women?**

A: That both men and women must be treated equally either in worship or social life.

1283. **Q: Who was the tenth Guru?**

A: Tegh Bahadurs son of Guru Gobind Singh. He was only nine-years-old but built up an effective army.

1284. **Q: What is the Holy book of Sikhs?**

A: Guru Granth Sahib (it contains hymns written by Guru) and the content was provided by all the ten Gurus, Hindu and Muslin scholars. It is also called Adi Granth.

1285. **Q: What is the main belief?**

A: That God does not belong to any faith and that God cannot be represented so images of God are meaningless. One could see God's spirit through mediation and sincere worship.

1286. **Q: What do they think of Gurus in relation to God?**

A: Sikhs believe that God's words were represented by God (or Guru being God representative) especially the ten Gurus.

1287. **Q: What do they think of the equality?**

A: They believe that men and women are equal.

1288. **Q: What is the meal after worship called?**

A: Langar (anyone is invited – Sikh and non-Sikh).

1289. **Q: What are their other beliefs?**

A: They believe in reincarnation, no training for priesthood to be trained to read the Holy script; death is regarded as the next stage of continuing one's life in another stage, they are encouraged to recite the funeral prayers before going to bed (Sohila Mohala).

1290. **Q: What else do they practice in their social lives?**

A: Sikhs are not allowed to smoke tobacco or take illicit drugs, drink alcohol, are vegetarian, must not gamble, steal, commit adultery and help others (charity).

1291. **Q: What about names given when someone is born?**

A: All the Sikh men have surnames (Singh "lion") and all female surnames are Kaur (princess).

1292. **Q: Describe the place of worship.**

A: Their worship place is called Gurdwara, which means door of the Guru, e.g. Golden Temple at Amritsar in the Punjab.

1293. **Q: How can one identify the building for worshipping?**

A: They are purpose-built, and all have the same features of shape and appearance.

1294. **Q: What other features or facilities?**

A: All Gurdwara's have kitchens to prepare the meal (Langer), eating room and classroom for children to be taught the Gurmukhi.

1295. **Q: What is the approximate number of followers?**

A: About 20 million.

1296. **Q: What are practising Sikhs advised to wear?**

A: Five K's: 1. Kesh; 2. Kangha; 3. Kara; 4. Kacha; and 5. Kirpan.

1297. **Q: What is Kesh?**

A: They must not cut their hair, men must cover their hair with a turban, but this is optional for women.

1298. **Q: What is Kangha?**

A: To keep the hair clean and neat by combing as an indication of the importance of cleanliness.

1299. **Q: What is Kara?**

A: To symbolise equality, Sikhs are encouraged to wear an iron or steel bracelet on the right wrist.

1300. **Q: What is Kacha or Kacchera?**

A: Sikhs must always wear shorts and suitable clothing for an active life as a symbol of morality.

1301. **Q: What is Kirpan?**

A: Sikhs are encouraged to have small swords and an emblem of power and dignity. This represents self-respect, fearlessness, protection of the weak and vulnerable in the society.

1302. **Q: How will you describe Sikhs?**

A: One who believes in one God, reads the Holy book known as Guru Granth Sahib and does not believe in any other God or rituals.

1303. **Q: When was the Holy book written?**

A: It was written by the tenth Guru Granth Sahib during the period 1469–1708.

1304. **Q: How are Sikh's names chosen, i.e. given name or first name?**

A: All Sikhs, whether male or female, must take one of these five names: 1. Mohinder; 2. Surinder; 3. Davinder; 4. Ranji; or 5. Hardeep.

1305. **Q: How do Sikhs choose a family name or surname?**

A: This will be a religious surname in accordance to the Sikh Code of Conduct.

1306. **Q: What is obligatory in choosing a surname?**

A: Guru Gobind Singh made it obligatory for male followers to call themselves Singh.

1307. **Q: What does Singh mean?**

A: Lion.

1308. **Q: What is obligatory for females?**

A: They must call themselves Kaur.

1309. **Q: What does Kaur mean?**

A: Princess. For example, Mohinder Singh or Ranji Kaur.

1310. **Q: Whom do Sikhs worship?**

A: They worship one Supreme God who communicates through the Gurus.

1311. **Q: Which country is more populated?**

A: Punjab.

1312. **Q: What are the five virtues of the Sikh religion?**

A: Truth, contentment, service, patience and humility.

1313. **Q: What do Sikhs regard as cardinal vices?**

A: Lust, anger, greed, worldliness and pride.

1314. **Q: Name the three commitments.**

A: Praying, working and giving.

1315. **Q: What is "Nam Japna"?**

A: Keeping in mind always.

1316. **Q: How is keeping in mind achieved?**

A: By meditation on God's name "Nam".

1317. **Q: What is Kirk Karma?**

A: To work hard and honestly, avoid gambling, begging and not to work in the alcohol or tobacco industries.

1318. **Q: What is Vand Chakna?**

A: To give alms – give to charity, care for others.

1319. **Q: What is Langer?**

A: It is a community meal to act of service.

1320. **Q: What is one of the most important Sikhs beliefs?**

A: That everybody is equal, be he a man or a woman, Sikh or non-Sikh, rich or poor.

1321. **Q: Who is Khalsa?**

A: It is a name given to an adult who is initiated as a Sikh.

1322. **Q: What are the main requirements of Sikhs?**

A: No adultery, no alcohol, no narcotics and not to worship any other God especially not to worship Hindu deities.

1323. **Q: What name is given to the sacred book?**

A: It is named after the "eleventh Guru" Granth Sahib.

1324. **Q: Name Sikh festivals.**

A:

a.	5th January	The birthday of Guru Gobind Singh
b.	14th April	Baisakhi/Vaisakhi
c.	16th June	Martyrdom of Guru Arjan Dev
d.	11th November	Bandi Chhor (Diwali)
e.	25th November	The birthday of Guru Nanek
f.	24th November	Commemoration of Guru Teg Bahadur
g.	1st September	First reading of Guru Granth Sahib
h.	20th October	Formal installation of Guru Granth Sahib as guidance for Sikhs.

Chapter 13

Taoism

1325. Q: Where did Taoism originate from and who is the key leader?

A: In China – it is the main leader. It originates from the sixth century 500BCE.

1326. Q: What is the main aim or philosophy?

A: To gain serenity, beyond the human conception of good and bad.

1327. Q: What is the meaning of Lao Tzu?

A: Tien-shih – heavenly master.

1328. Q: What are the other doctrines?

A: Produce and maintain without desire, intention and struggle.

1329. Q: What is Tao's main characteristic?

A: Seek liberation from any constraint, being political, mortality.

1330. Q: How?

A: This had caused political differences from various governments but the changes of some had taken its toll on the integrity of the state government.

1331. **Q: What other main religion/faith overlaps Taoism?**

A: Buddhism.

1332. **Q: Quote a speech or text from the Taoist practice.**

A: In the pursuit of learning, every day something is acquired. In the pursuit of Tao, every day something is discarded. The world is ruled by letting things take their course. It cannot be ruled by interfering. (Lao-Tzu, Tao Te Ching).

1333. **Q: How do Taoists achieve their God?**

A: The ability to live at ease is to encourage an understanding of the natural balance and harmony of all things.

1334. **Q: What method is used to sustain these?**

A: The protocol is to believe in meditation and the use of breathing techniques to achieve or develop self.

1335. **Q: How many members were there after the year 2000?**

A: Over 20 million worldwide.

1336. **Q: Name the typical concept of Taoism.**

A: They believe in the other side of tradition and Chinese culture with ideas of "Yin" and "Yang" known as the five elements.

1337. **Q: What is Tai Chi?**

A: This is termed as the Great Ultimate consisting of a series of 108 complex slow movements and this are respected by the Chinese and other countries worldwide.

1338. **Q: What is the Tao religion?**

A: It started in China (1200BC)

1339. **Q: Who are the main two leaders?**

A: Laozi in the sixth century and Zhuang Zi in the fourth century.

1340. **Q: Do they believe in God?**

A: They believe that there is a supreme being who created humans, the universe and spirit.

1341. **Q: What is the name of their philosophy book?**

A: Zhang Dao.

1342. **Q: Who founded Taoism?**

A: Laozi.

1343. **Q: Why did he used to ride an ox?**

A: It symbolises the start of the new year.

1344. **Q: Tell us one dream of Zhuang Zi.**

A: "Once upon a time, I, Zhuang Zi dreamt that I was a butterfly, flitting around and enjoying myself. I had no idea I was Zhuang Zi. Then suddenly I woke up and was Zhuang Zi again. But I could not tell, had I been Zhuang Zi. Dreaming I was a butterfly, or a butterfly dreaming I was now Zhuang Zi."

Chapter 14

Zoroastrian

1345. **Q: What is Zoroastrian and when and where did it start?**

A: It was believed to have started or was named after Prophet Zoroaster in about 1200BCE, in ancient Persia. It is a religion.

1346. **Q: Why did Zoroaster start this religion?**

A: It is believed that he had various visions and his opposition to sacrifice and hallucinogenic or rituals.

1347. **Q: How is the state of Persia involved?**

A: The Persian empire was established by Achaemenes in about the sixth century. Zoroastrianism was acknowledged as the main religion (600–650BCE).

1348. **Q: What happened when the Arabs and Islamist forces overran the Persian empire in 650BCE?**

A: Those Zoroastrian's who refused to convert or retreat were persecuted.

1349. **Q: What happened to those who remained alive?**

A: They were in and around Iran and continued their faith as Zoroastrians but changed the name to Mazdayasnians or worshippers of God.

1350. **Q: What name was given to those who settled in India?**

A: In the tenth century the Zoroastrians escaped to India and called themselves Parsees or "Persians".

1351. **Q: What happened to Zoroastrians when the Islamic resolution took place in Iran?**

A: Most of the Iranian Zoroastrians emigrated to establish themselves in Canada and California.

1352. **Q: What is the Zoroastrian Holy book called?**

A: It is called Avesta and consists of a collection of hymns and information called "Gathas".

1353. **Q: What is their philosophy?**

A: Worship the "Wise Lord" or Ahura Mazda – all goodness is to be focused on a good spirit known as "Spenta Mainyu".

1354. **Q: Do they have evil spirits?**

A: Yes, they call it "Destructive Spirit" or Angra Mainy.

1355. **Q: Where do they stand with regards to God?**

A: They were one of the monotheistic; the members have free will of choice between good and evil.

1356. **Q: What do they strive for?**

A: Their belief in God is that if you do good, you will reap the rewards of happiness on earth and eventually go to Heaven, but the wicked, liars, deceitful and evil people will end up in Hell.

1357. **Q: How would you describe Zoroastrians?**

A: They aim for higher morals, concepts, are very optimistic but deterred from any form of evil in this world.

1358. **Q: What is the name of their priest?**

A: The priest is known as "dastur mobed" or mogh or magi.

1359. **Q: How are the priests initiated?**

A: The initiation is called sedreh pushi or navjote, they put on a sacred cord (koshti) and a white shirt (sedreh) as a reminder to fight or avoid evil.

1360. **Q: How are they used to dispose of their dead?**

A: The procedure is to expose the dead corpse to birds and animals in what they used to call Towers of Silence. This has stopped.

1361. **Q: What do they have in their worship place?**

A: No statues or images; they worship almighty God by meditating and focus on fire.

1362. **Q: What does the fire symbolise and their religion symbol?**

A: The fire symbolises "purity" and the symbol stand for "Fravahar" – wide-winged bird.

1363. **Q: What does Fravahar stand for?**

A: It is believed to stand for far or presence of wisdom in God.

1364. **Q: Do the Zoroastrians have influence on other faiths?**

A: Yes, they include Judaism, Christianity, Foreshadowing, Judgement day, Heaven and Hell, and are believed to be found in the Bible Ezekiel and Nimrod.

References

Abdullah Yusuf Ali (Translate) (2001) *The Holy Quran: Transliteration in Roman Script with Arabic Text and English Translation*, Kitab Bhavan.

Ahalya Gautam (2017) *Guru Gobind Singh*, Independently published.

Ancient and Accepted Scottish Rile of Freemasonry. Washington, DC: Southern Jurisdiction 1794–1976.

Author unknown (2016*) HOLY BIBLE: King James Version (KJV) White Presentation Edition (Kjv Bible)*, William Collins; UK ed. Edition.

Bullock, Stephen C. *The Revolutionary Transformation of American Freemason 1752–1792* by William and Mary Quarterly.

Claudy, Car H. (1931) *Introduction of Freemason Master Mason.* Washington, DC: The Temple Publisher. Clausen, Henry.

Claudy, Car H. (1931) *Introduction to Freemason: Fellowcraft.* Washington, DC: The Temple Publisher. Clausen, Henry.

Claudy, Carl H. *Introduction to Freemasonry: Entered Apprentice*. Washington, DC: The Temple Publisher.

Clausen, Henry *38° Severing Grand Commander. Clausen's Commentaries on Morals and Dogma Supreme Council 33 Degree*.

Coil, Henry Wilson (2011) *Coil's Masonic Encyclopaedia*. Macoy Publishing a Masonic supply, Co. Inc.

Encyclopaedia of Freemason: The Masonic History Company 1912.

Freemason symbol pictures obtained from the Internet.

Jeffers, Paul (2005) *Freemasons Inside the World's Oldest Secret Society*. Kensington Publishing Corp: Citadel Press Books.

Knight, S. (1984) *The Brotherhood: The Secret World of the Freemasons*. Dorset Press.

Mackey, Albert Gallatin (2008) *The History of Freemasonry, Its Legendary Origins*. Dover Publications.

Macoy, Robert (2000) *A Dictionary of Freemason Gramercy Books.* Random House Value Publishing.

Naudon, Paul (1991) *the Secret History of Freemasonry: It's Origins and Connection to the Knights Templar.* Rochester: Inner Traditions. Vermont.

Newton, Joseph F. (1973) *The Builders. The Supreme Council 33rd Degree.* Lexington, Massachusetts: AA&R.

Random House Value Publishing 1966 McKays Revised.

Short, Martin (1990) *Inside the Brotherhood: Further Secret of the Freemasons.* Dorset Press.

Sivananda Swami (2010) *The Bhagavad Gita,* The Divine Life Society.

Index

A

Abraham, 6, 76, 100, 103, 104, 243, 249, 264, 265, 267, 282, 295, 296, 361

Abu, 244, 245, 246, 247, 307, 308, 316

Advent, 66

Allah, 2, 62, 63, 97, 98, 99, 206, 230, 235, 236, 237, 238, 239, 240, 241, 242, 243, 248, 249, 250, 251, 252, 253, 255, 256, 257, 258, 259, 260, 271, 272, 274, 275, 276, 280, 282, 283, 284, 285, 291, 292, 293, 294, 295, 298, 300, 303, 304, 306, 310, 311, 312, 313, 314, 315, 316, 317, 318, 319, 320, 321, 322

Amaterasu, 379

Amos, 75

angel, 95, 106

Anglican, 66, 67, 69, 110

apocalypse, 359

Arabs, 245, 256, 259, 261, 262, 398

Ark, ix, 205, 359, 363, 365

Asatru, 374

Ascension, 67, 71, 234

Ashurg, 233

Atma, 198, 204, 224, 225, 226

Aum, 198

Avatars, 110, 193, 209

B

Baha, 1, 2, 3, 4, 5, 6, 7, 266, 269

Baha'i, 1, 2, 4, 5, 6, 269

Baptist, 67, 80, 105, 106, 249, 267

belief, 87, 88, 93

Bhagavad-Gita, 192, 217

bhakti, 51, 214

C

D

408

H

409

212, 214, 217, 218, 353, 386, 393

Holi, 195, 203, 204, 216

Hosea, 75

I

Iman, 233

Isaac, 100, 236, 249, 361

Isaiah, 74, 116, 121

Ishmael, 100, 249, 265

Israelites, 88

J

Jacob, 100

Jainism, 351, 352, 354, 355

James, 72, 76, 77, 79, 82, 93, 107, 110, 112, 113, 114, 115, 117, 119, 120, 121

Jehovah, 67, 105, 257

Jeremiah, 74, 118, 121

Jerusalem, 65

Jesus, viii, 6, 8, 11, 30, 59, 63, 64, 65, 66, 67, 68, 69, 70, 71, 73, 76, 77, 78, 83, 92, 95, 97, 98, 99, 100, 101, 103, 105, 106, 107, 108, 109, 110, 111, 112, 113, 114, 117, 123, 150, 151, 152, 153, 154, 155, 206, 230, 231, 248, 249, 253, 254, 256, 257, 264,266, 267, 268, 269, 284, 286, 287, 288, 290, 294, 295, 296, 297, 298, 299, 301, 302, 303, 305, 307, 309, 317, 323

Jesus Christ, 78

Jews, 253, 254, 257, 259, 262, 268, 269, 305, 359, 361, 362, 364, 366, 367, 368, 369, 370, 371

jiva, 356

Job, 75, 100, 121, 236, 243, 249, 258

Joel, 75

John, 67, 68, 75, 76, 78, 79, 101, 105, 106, 107, 108, 117, 121, 123

Jonah, 74, 75, 100, 121

410

M

Maha Shivaratri, 195, 215

Mahabharata, 192, 197, 200, 212

Mala, 194

Malachi, 75

mandala, 52

mandir, 207, 208

Mantra, 200, 208

Marcus Garvey, 87

Mary, 66, 68, 77, 106, 107, 124, 323

master, 59, 99

meditation, 17, 22, 31, 39, 46, 50, 52, 203, 208, 211, 214, 374, 392, 395

Mesopotamia, 76, 361

messenger, 1, 3, 7, 99, 100, 240, 263, 306, 318, 319, 321, 382

Methodist, 66, 67, 78, 110

Micah, 75

miracles, 11, 66, 72, 99, 107, 109, 111, 369

Mirza, 3, 5

Moksha, 190, 205, 352, 354

Monks, 29, 48

Moses, vii, 6, 30, 74, 100, 169, 231, 243, 248, 249, 253, 254, 257, 264, 268, 323, 360, 362, 363, 367, 369

mother, 65, 77, 106, 124

Muhammad, viii, 2, 5, 6, 7, 11, 30, 99, 101, 103, 111, 154, 194, 206, 230, 231, 233, 234, 235, 236, 237, 238, 240, 242, 244, 245, 247, 249, 250, 252, 254, 256, 257, 259, 261, 262, 263, 264, 265, 267, 268, 269, 270, 271, 279, 282, 285, 289, 290, 291, 295, 303, 304, 306, 307, 308, 309, 311, 313, 314, 316, 321

Muharran, 233

Murti, 194

Muslim, 99, 231, 232, 235, 236, 242, 250, 252, 253, 259, 260, 262, 268, 286, 293, 301, 306, 309, 311, 323, 386

412

mystical, 92

N

Nahum, 75

Nam Japna, 392

Nanak, 382, 386

Navarotri, 195

Nehemiah, 75

New Testament, 75

Nicodemus, 123

Nirvana, 23, 41, 42, 47

Noah, 100

Noble truths, 49

Nuns, 48, 260

O

Obadiah, 75

Odinism, 374

Old Testament, 72, 74, 75, 76

Orthodox, 66, 67, 365, 369, 370

P

Pagan, 372, 373, 374, 376, 377

Pali, 15, 18, 56

Palki, 385

Panjab, 383, 384

paradise, 98

Pasryushana, 356

Passover, 368, 369

Pentecost, 67, 71

Persia, 362, 398

Peter, 76, 108

Pharaoh, ix, 233, 253

Philemon, 76

Philippians, 75

Pilate, 63

pillars, 163, 186, 263, 275, 361

posture, 1, 60, 103, 275, 277, 278, 279, 280, 281, 282, 283

Protestant, 68, 69

Proverbs, 75

Psalms, 75, 81, 99

414

Printed in Great Britain
by Amazon